# 22 YEARS
## A KASHMIR STORY
### ONE LAKH PANDIT FAMILIES MAY HAVE ONE LAKH STORIES

**BILL K KOUL**

Vitasta
LET KNOWLEDGE SPREAD

Published by
Renu Kaul Verma
Vitasta Publishing Pvt Ltd
2/15, Ansari Road, Daryaganj
New Delhi - 110 002
info@vitastapublishing.com

ISBN 978-93-86473-14-1
© Bill K Koul, 2018
Reprint 2018

All Rights Reserved.
No part of this publication may be reproduced, stored in a retrieval system, or transmitted in any form, or by any means—electronic, mechanical, photocopying, recording or otherwise—without the prior permission of the publisher.

Cover and layout by Vits Press
Printed by Vikas Computer and Printers

# 22YEARS
## A KASHMIR STORY

This book is dedicated to Jai Kishori Koul (*Rani*), my mother, for giving birth to me, her personal sacrifices, human values, unconditional love for all; and for everything that she was for me and did for me; and

To Bansi Lal Hakhu (*Bhaisahib*), my Guru, the spiritual father, for pulling me out of the wilderness and mental abyss; for resuscitating and resurrecting me by initiating me into Transcendental Meditation (TM); for his fatherly love, wise words and regular teachings; and for my spiritual awakening.

My eternal gratitude to both; without their love and efforts, I would not have existed.

I dedicate this book to all Kashmiris.

# Contents

*Preface* — ix
*Who am I?* — xix
*Acknowledgements* — xxv

The Son Comes Home — 1
The Day of Exile — 31
The Years Before the Exit — 38
Life in Kashmir — 66
A Refugee in India—Jammu & Delhi — 106
Cultural Transition & Challenges — 135
Conversations in Wilderness — 161

# Preface

This book tells an inspiring true story about a Kashmiri boy who defied numerous odds to survive and find his way back into the world. He survived a difficult caesarean childbirth, being a breech baby; grew up as the only child of his parents; saw his family being excommunicated and ostracised when his eldest aunt married a Muslim when he was just about eight years old; could not spell a word of English or know the tables till the age of ten, but still figured amongst the rank holders in his Year 10 and Year 11 Examinations; miraculously survived an acute gastroenteritis attack barely two days before his *viva-voce* examination for admission to an engineering college when he was still shy of his 16th birthday; got uprooted from his homeland (Kashmir) due to an unprecedented political upheaval when he was about 27 years old, following which he took a vow that he would never return to his homeland; moved across three countries between the ages of 32 and 40, starting from scratch five times during that period of eight years.

And it so happened one day, as destiny would have it, that he returned to his homeland, albeit for only a couple of days, after a period of 22 years.

The reasons underlying his sudden, unplanned and unexpected flying return visit to Kashmir illustrate the nature and the state of his mind, which over the years has changed from a sad and rather despondent childhood; to relative happiness and promise during his teenage years; to a heartbreak as a young man; to extreme anxiety, fear and depression during the months leading to the mass exodus of his community from Kashmir; back to utter despondency and extreme anger in the period immediately following the mass exodus; to anxiety and continued struggle for achieving some dignity and stability in life; and finally to compassion and empathy for the world community. Such has been the life journey of this rather enigmatic person; an absolute roller coaster. And that person is the author of this book.

Life is full of surprises. With age, generally, people become nostalgic about their childhood world. I am no different. The memories of my childhood, and my world during those precious days, my grandparents and the family home, relatives, neighbours and friends, often transport me mentally back in time to the land where I was born and raised, and where all my ancestors were born and raised. With time, the nostalgia has grown and with that my newly-found attachment and the affinity to that land has also grown. That land is Kashmir, my homeland. I am a son of the soil, similar to my father and grandfather, and all our ancestors. I believe that I owe a great deal to my homeland and her people.

This book is not a work of fiction. It is based on my own observations, thoughts, life experience and real events. This book has not been intended to contain any significant political content, whatsoever. However, for the completion of my memoirs, reference to the political uprising of 1990 in Kashmir, has been deemed necessary and unavoidable. Similarly, the basic philosophy in support of the return of Pandits to the valley has been included in this book.

I lived with my family in Kashmir till our sudden and painful migration from the valley in December 1989. The book has been inspired by my sudden and short return visit to Kashmir in April 2012. This book illustrates my story—the story of a migrant Kashmiri Pandit, who is now a citizen of the world.

The first draft of the book was titled *Twenty-three Years* to mark the time period of my absence from Kashmir. However, my last visit to Kashmir, in July 2016, and the volatile conditions that I witnessed there, made me to change the title to *22 Years*. In my opinion, Kashmir is suffering and bleeding from a *Catch 22* situation. The new title of the book also fits in well with my passion about the game of cricket, where a bat battles with a ball over a distance of 22 yards and 22 players play the game.

The mass exodus of the Pandits from the valley in 1990 physically separated the two Kashmiri communities, the Hindus and the Muslims but not their memories of each other. After all, they are one ethnic Kashmiri people—people who share a common ancestry, speak the same language, eat the same food and are related by blood. However, our younger generations have been left deprived of that life experience of being able to live in an interwoven social fabric, which was characterised by a considerable interdependence of the two communities. The younger generation of the two communities, born in the valley and outside it, cannot be blamed for being generally ignorant about how the life of the two communities was intertwined in the past. People born after 1986, especially during 1990 or 1991, will have absolutely no memory of the sudden exodus of the Pandits, the indigenous people of Kashmir. This means that Kashmiri youth, including my own children, will currently have only a transmitted memory but not a real memory of the pre-1990 interwoven social fabric. My story may provide them with a glimpse into our past life in Kashmir. I hope and pray that this story helps to stitch the social fabric of our Kashmiri community back together and produce a beautiful tapestry about a land which was once called 'heaven on earth'.

The first half of the book provides a glimpse into my personal life experiences.

The second half of the book presents my political, philosophical and spiritual perspectives about Kashmir and the world at large, as well as a commentary on a wide range of issues, which in my opinion, currently confront Kashmir and the wider world such as:

> Why is it important to address Kashmir's ecological, environmental, cultural and political issues?
> Why is it important to expand love and universal brotherhood to combat the current menace of hate and violence around the world; and how daily practice of meditation by the people can help to achieve a much desired state of world peace and stability?
> Why is it extremely important to address the gender bias in all communities around the world and why women must have equal representation in each and every walk of life?

In the last chapter of this book, I have reproduced my recent conversations, on a popular social media application, with a number of people from both Kashmiri Muslim and Pandit communities. The intent is to provide a snapshot of an average current Kashmiri mindset.

I believe that numerous violent incidents and human deaths that are currently occurring around the world, almost on a daily basis, are the result of a dire paucity of love which the humans are currently experiencing. By nature, humans strive for love and attention and, if they do not receive that, they react with hate and anger. I consider that, before it is too late, both women and men of substance and those in power must consciously put in a coordinated and determined effort to bring all women at par with their male counterparts where they live and work. Full empowerment of women is the call of the hour.

A man generally symbolises physical strength and anger, whereas a woman generally symbolises love and nurturing. In my strong opinion, the key to world peace, stability and sustainability is the empowerment of the women to bring them at par with their male counterparts in all aspects of life. Women represent half of the human species on this earth. Without them, life on earth is not possible. They are biologically stronger than men in terms of their longevity, resilience and tenacity. As long as women, who are considered the embodiment of love, care and nurturing, are not treated with full dignity and respect, it is very difficult, if not impossible, to expand universal love and harmony between various people.

As for Kashmir, I believe that, for peace to return to Kashmir, the present day inhabitants of the valley must reconnect with their roots in Sufism and Kashmiri Shaivism thought. The key to the return of peace to the valley is in the return of Pandits to the valley. The Pandits are the original inhabitants of the valley and have been living there long before the advent of Islam. The Pandits that lived in the valley up to 1990 are the direct descendants of those Kashmiris who had stuck to the original faith of their ancestors even though many of their Pandit ancestors had converted to Islam during the last half a millennium or so, for a range of reasons.

Contrary to a popular thought in modern day Kashmir, Pandits are not, and have never been, cowards. Instead they were peaceful, soft and gentle. None of these qualities reflects weakness; these terms reflect virtues, which were their strengths. To show one's strength, one does not have to carry a gun or a sword or shout abuse! They and their Pandit ancestors had historically survived in Kashmir against numerous odds. Conversion to Islam would have always been an easier option for them; however, they had always chosen the harder path sticking to their roots and the faith of their ancestors. Cowardice is not saving one's life and honour in the face of an armed aggression; cowardice is to show aggression to unarmed peace-loving and virtuous people.

I liken the various Kashmiri communities to the branches of a tree, including the grafted branches; all of which receive nourishment from the common roots of that tree. Alien trees generally don't bear fruit in Kashmir; it is prudent to replant and nourish the native trees instead. For their peace, survival and growth, Kashmiris must look for their roots and nourish themselves with traditional Kashmiri values and spirituality.

The roots of spirituality in Kashmir lie in Kashmiri Shaivism, whose proponents and practitioners are Kashmir's Pandits. It is very important, therefore, to recognise that the much-needed role of Kashmiri Pandits in Kashmir will be to provide the hyphen Kashmiris with a connection with their original spiritual roots. Therefore, so long as Kashmiri Pandits don't return to Kashmir and reinstate the tapestry of Kashmiri culture and spirituality, the return of peace to the valley seems to be remote. A piece of cloth cannot be stitched without a thread. Similar to a thread, Pandits will help to reinstate the unique Kashmiri tapestry.

Well, it is another thing if the Pandits will ever return, given the level of distrust in their mind! Pandits are not, and have not, been at the mercy of anyone; they chose to leave the valley out of their own volition and their decision to return to the valley will always be their own.

Historically, Pandits have never followed any religious or a political leader slavishly. Being an extremely intelligent, evolved and proud community, Pandits are characteristically individualistic. Therefore, they follow their own judgement and act individually. In some extreme situations though or in scenarios of common interest, their actions may coincidentally appear to be aligned and synchronised.

As such, as far as the matter of Kashmiri Pandits' return to the valley is concerned, the onus should logically be on Pandits, ie. if, when and how they wish to return. Most importantly, Pandits must never return until and unless all their Muslim brethren and their leadership sincerely and unconditionally request them to do so.

Having tasted freedom after their exodus from the valley, it is inconceivable that all Pandits will ever consider returning to the valley, given a continued strife there. They are currently scattered all over the planet and moving ahead with their regular lives. If anyone actually decides to return, it will practically be a gift for the valley. The present inhabitants of the valley will do themselves and their homeland a big favour by welcoming those individuals.

> *Life is not fair;*
> *be kind to yourself and to the other person for whom you care.*
> *If you are hard on yourself, you may be hard on others as well,*
> *not knowing how many of them could also be*
> *living their own hell.*
> —Bill K Koul

This book has not been written without undergoing some degree of scrutiny and challenges from my family. During the early days of my writing this book, my daughter, Deeksha, suddenly commented, 'Papa, I know you are good at writing technical reports, but writing a book of this type is another thing. You don't read much. You may really embarrass yourself. You ought to have undertaken a thorough research before starting to write this book. Writers usually take years to write a book after undertaking a detailed research on the topic they write.'

'Deeksha, fair enough, but I am not writing the history of Kashmir. I intend to write only what is and has been in my head. It is all there (pointing to my head). I am trying to download my thoughts and memories into this book. If I don't document them, we'll lose them and no one will ever know what was inside my head. I am not writing a historical, political or a social commentary. It is my story', I replied.

'But who is going to read your book?' Deeksha asked.

'I expect all Kashmiris to read it, from both Pandit and Muslim communities', I replied.

'Why do you try to separate the two communities?' she asked, sounding somewhat confused.

'I am not trying to separate them. I am trying to acknowledge both communities for their respective roles, as they comprise the entire Kashmiri community. It is like describing a tapestry which has been weaved using two threads that are made from the same material but differently shaded and coloured', I clarified.

'But why should people be actually interested in knowing your story and bother to read this book?' Deeksha probed.

I replied, 'Because people are likely to correlate their personal stories with my story. Every individual carries a story in his/her head. There could be possibly hundreds of people out there who may have similar stories, but for some reason they chose not to write them and share it with others. My mother enjoyed listening to sad filmi songs and watching movies with relatively sad and tragic themes, just because she was not very happy inside. Sad songs and sad movies would probably provide vent to her emotions. Similarly, I believe there will be many people who would possibly relate to my story and provide vent to their feelings. Let me write for them, let it be their voice too!'

During the writing phase of this book, the whole world, including myself, seemed to be working against me, with a coordinated and concerted plan, and thwarting my painstaking effort. Similar to my life, the writing process of this book was also an absolute emotional roller coaster for me. I relived a concentrated form of my past life. Every time I provided an account of a painful past event, my emotional injuries refreshed. I had to endure and overcome a significant amount of mental pain to be able to finish writing this book. In addition, I had to battle numerous serious distractions and issues from a number of sources, all beyond my reasonable control. These distractions had the potential to seriously undermine my energy and inspiration to write. I realised that it was one of those 'now or never' cases, where any disruption or loss of momentum would seriously jeopardise my attempt to complete this work. So I kept inching ahead into a strong head wind, albeit with much lesser momentum at times. I had strong faith and felt that someone was indeed watching over me!

This book was originally inspired in late 2015 by Manoj Kaul, when he was in Perth and before he returned to Houston, Texas, US. Thereafter, on 17 March 2016, a fellow meditator, Rakesh Safaya, encouraged me to write a book on TM and how it had changed my life. Its start was triggered by a gentle reminder at Boston by my cousin, Sanjay Kaul.

## Who am I?

In this book, for convenience, I have referred to myself as *Billu*, as a third person.

I have been known by several names. Billu is the original name, by which I have been called by my father's family after my birth and I have known myself before my schooling started. Our relatives from my father's side call me by this name; however, my relatives from my maternal side call me *Gitton*. The name is after a British gentleman, one Mr Gitton, who was a close friend of my maternal grandfather. Years later, at the time of my school admission, in 1969, I was registered initially as *Deepak Koul*, which was changed to *Kuldeep Kumar Koul* in 1971.

In the Australian consulting engineering industry, I am known as *Bill Koul*, which actually is a shortened version of my original name at home, *Billu*. I am aware about some degree of criticism from some of my orthodox Kashmiri and Indian friends and relatives about my adoption of a westernised name for work purposes. As is a common practice in the western countries, people prefer to adopt short names for ease of communication. My adopted name has allowed my clients and industry peers to focus more on work related matters with me rather than get curious about my background, etc. Also, it has saved me from painful distortions of my registered name, which I had experienced earlier in Malaysia, where I lived with my family for several years prior to moving to Australia. In Malaysia also, I worked in the local geotechnical consulting engineering industry. In business related communications and correspondences, it was not uncommon to find my name being misspelt, rather distorted, such as Kudip, Kudit, Gudit, Gudip etc. Hence, on the back of my Malaysian learning, to save further distortions of my registered name and the pain associated with it, I decided to keep it simple in Australia. It has also given me a more universal identity!

I was born and raised in a Kashmiri Pandit family in Srinagar, Kashmir. Up to 1982, we lived at Alikadal, near Wazapora, in downtown Srinagar and, thereafter, moved to a newly constructed family house within a new residential colony at Rawalpora.

I was born in the Koul family of Malchamar (in downtown Alikadal) in the early sixties. Our family is uniquely nicknamed as *Ladakhi*. Anecdotally, several past generations lived in Ladakh, the northernmost part of the Jammu & Kashmir state. Pandit Kanwal Koul was the first generation of my family who returned to Srinagar on the then Maharaja's invitation. He was appointed as *vazir-e-vazarat* by the Maharaja. His descendants were Pandit Chitraj Koul, Pandit Ishwar Koul and Pandit Sona Koul and then my grandfather Pandit Shamboo Nath Koul. Our first ancestral home in Srinagar was located at Babapora, in Habba Kadal, where three generations of my ancestors lived before moving to Alikadal. That building was subsequently converted into the Babapora High School.

I am the only child of Jai Kishori Koul (*Rani*) and Jawahar Lal Koul (*Boba*). Rani was a homemaker throughout her life. Boba is a civil engineer by profession; he retired in 2002 as the Chief Engineer, PWD Kashmir.

My grandmother, Dhanwati Koul (*Amaji*), was born in the Kadalbajoo family of Gurgari Mohalla, Alikadal, to Pandit

Tika Lal Kadalbajoo and Zoonmal Kadalbajoo. My paternal grandfather, Shamboo Nath Koul (*Tathaji*), was a high school teacher. He enjoyed great repute in his time as a teacher of Mathematics and English.

My maternal grandmother was Lilawati Kaul (*Kaki*). My maternal grandfather, Pandit Niranjan Nath Kaul (*Pitaji*) of Gurgari Mohalla, Alikadal, worked for the Department of Tourism as a Tourist Officer before his untimely demise, in 1966, at the age of 53 years. I have only a very faint and hazy memory of Pitaji sitting by a window, with a warm smile on his face.

At the time of our departure from Kashmir in 1989, I was about 27 years old and had been married for about three years to Rekha Bhan, daughter of Sheilaji and Radha Krishan Bhan, with a two year old son, Kongposh (*Baba*). Our daughter, Deeksha (*Shang-e-Asham*) was born in Jammu on the Christmas Day of 1990.

My life has been full of ups and downs, mostly downs. It has been like a necklace of thorny beads, with occasional rounded ones.

My personal religious philosophy may not be exactly in line with those members of both Pandit and Muslim community who possess and profess extreme interpretations of their respective religious mindsets. I have been susceptible to apprehensions and doubts from the right wing members belonging to both communities to such an extent that some Pandits may currently be regarding me as a half-Hindu and a half-Muslim, whereas some Muslims may be regarding me as an extremely fundamental kind of Hindu. In practical terms, being a vegetarian / vegan, I don't see much difference between the two communities; both eat and relish non-vegetarian food, speak the same language and share numerous cultural traits, and are related by blood.

In my opinion, how people say farewell to their dead or pray to their god do not make the two Kashmiri communities significantly different, or for that matter any world communities different from one another.

As for religion, I believe every individual has his / her own religious understanding, interpretation and the general philosophy about this life and the world hereafter. Those differences exist between members of a family, between siblings, between a husband and a wife, between parents and their children, between two bosom friends.

> *Bannaa chahata hun ek achha insaan,*
> *na ki Hindu ya Musalman;*
> *karta hun roz dhyan, taki banu ek achha insaan!*
> I want to be a good human being and not a
> Hindu or a Muslim.
> I meditate daily so that I become a good human being.
> — Bill K Koul

My religious philosophy is uniquely my own and a resultant of my experience, observations, contemplation and the inspiration derived from great prophets and saints. To put it simply, it is a blend of Kashmiri Sufism, Jainism, Buddhism, Sikhism, Christianity and Hinduism.

I have been inspired, not in any particular order, by:

> Gurudev Brahmanand Saraswati and his esteemed disciple Maharishi Mahesh Yogi, who gave this world the technique of Transcendental Meditation (TM);
> Lord Ram (The *Purshottam*, ie. the perfect man), as illustrated in the Hindu epic Ramayana, for whom my deep reverence and devotion was sown and nurtured by my Guru, Bhaisahib;
> All ten Sikh Gurus, in particular Guru Teg Bahadurji, who offered supreme sacrifice for the cause of Kashmiri Pandits;

Noble teachings of Islam, as interpreted and described to me by my uncle, Abujan;

Jesus Christ and his noble teachings, in particular his supreme message of *forgiveness, compassion* and *love* for mankind;

Mahavir Jain for his message on non-violence and preservation of all life forms on this planet;

Gautam Buddha for spirituality and the Eight Fold Path;

Abraham Lincoln for being centuries ahead of his time and his lifelong fight for social justice, human rights and equality between all human beings; and

Mahatma Gandhi (Bapu) for his non-violent fight against injustice and self-service, simplicity, determination, resilience and tenacity.

I have been inspired by Lal Ded (Lalleshwari), who was a poetess from Kashmir in the 14th century and a very strong proponent of Shaivism, for which Kashmir is known through the world. Her mystic poetry has survived the last six hundred years and lived through oral recitations by numerous generations of Kashmiris. Her hymns poems, called *Lal vachhun* or Lal *vakhs* (words, sayings), influenced various Kashmiri Sufi saints, which include the famous Sheikh Noor-ud-din Wali (*Nunda Rishi)*.

Several Persian scholars and poets have also influenced my thought and spiritual space. These include: Abu-Muhammad Muslih al-Din bin Abdallah Shirazi (1210-1292), known popularly by his pen name as Sa'di and also as Sa'di of Shiraz, widely recognised as one of the greatest poets of the classical literary tradition. He is an internationally recognised and referred poet for the very high quality of his writings, the simplicity in the language and the depth of his social and moral thoughts. His poem collections are documented in two of his most famous books, *Bustan* and *Gulistan.* Jalal ad-Din Muhammad Rumi (1207–1273), popularly known as Rumi. He was a very popular poet, jurist, Islamic scholar, theologian and Sufi mystic. Khwaja Shams-ud-Din

Muhammad Hafez-e-Shirazi (1325/26–1389/90), known by his pen name Hafez, who was a Persian poet, whose works have deeply influenced the common person in Iran even today. His collected works, as documented in *The Divan of Hafez*, are regarded as a pinnacle of Persian literature. He is considered as the most influential of all Persians poets.

It is important to note that Kashmiris and Persians share strong cultural similarities and perhaps a common history in the distant past. Kashmiri Pandits mark their New Year around the spring equinox and term their New Year day as *Navreh*. Persians term their New Year day as *Navroz*. It is believed that old Kashmiri immigrants in the rest of India also call their new year day as *Navroz*. Both communities mark their new year day morning by looking into a *thaal* (a large plate), filled with dry rice and a number of other items, including a small mirror, pen and inkpot etc.; the Pandits call this ritual as *thaalbarun*.

The game of cricket has been my second religion. In so many ways, the game replicates life in general. Very early in my life, the game instilled the spirit of sportsmanship in me and taught me how to manage both loss and win on the field with dignity. The nature of the game trained me how to handle ups and downs in life. I also learnt the importance of showing respect towards one's opponents and acceptance of the umpire's decision without showing dissent even if one believes the umpire's decision is wrong. In cricket, anything can happen anytime; the game is generally quite unpredictable. The fortunes of a player can change within a few seconds. Therefore, all great cricket players remain humble, cool and level headed throughout their playing career, and in life in general.

Since my childhood, I have been fond of reading comic books. My favourite character has been *Phantom, the Ghost who walks*, by Lee Falk. Of all the popular comic characters, Phantom has perhaps been the only character who is not shown as a superhuman. His character is a mortal, with high morality and reliance.

# Acknowledgements

My gratitude and sincere thanks go to:

My father, Jawahar Lal Koul (*Boba*) for his invaluable support to me as my father and for my upbringing; having an optimistic mindset and humour; for showing, by example, the role of a son and a brother to one's sisters; service to the people; and choosing civil engineering as my profession;

My maternal uncle, Dr Avtar Krishan Kaul (*Boba Maama*), for his unconditional love and affection; for being a great story teller and introducing me to the world of imagination; for teaching me a number of board games; taking my early childhood pictures; and supporting my mother and me through our difficult days;

My paternal grandmother, Dhanwati Koul (*Amaji*), for bringing me up, her love and care and my introduction to the first written alphabet;

My paternal grandfather, Shamboo Nath Koul (*Tathaji*), for his simplicity and upright personality and providing inspiration, being the first torch bearer in the Koul family to follow the path of education; for his mastery of English literature, introducing plays of Shakespeare; and mastery in Mathematics; and service to the people;

My maternal grandmother, Lilawati Kaul (*Kaki*), for her boundless love, hard work, and dedication to all her children;

My maternal grandfather, Niranjan Nath Kaul (*Pitaji*), for genetically transmitting the colour of his eyes and his westernised thoughts and outlook into me;

My Guru Mata, Bimlaji Hakhu (*Mummyji*) for her unconditional and boundless love; her patience, tolerance and wisdom, and her motherly dedication to a large TM family;

My eldest aunt, Behanji, for being much ahead of her time and inculcating a forward looking approach in the Koul family, wisdom, guidance and for stepping into my mother's role after the loss of my mother;

My eldest uncle, Mufti Nazir Ahmad Farooqui (*Abujan*), for being a role model for me throughout my life; his uprightness and honesty; and for demonstrating, by example, how a family man should lead his life, as well as how to be socially responsible; his wise words and support to the Koul family, in particular at the time and after my mother's demise; and service to the people;

All my friends, in particular, Subash Kakroo, for our spiritual interaction and discourses; my colleague from Iran, Payam Sadeghi, for his simplicity and wise thoughts, our great philosophical chats during lunchtime at our workplace and for introducing me to such great mystic Persian poets as Sa'di, Rumi and Hafez; and Alex Ting for his assistance in formatting the manuscript. I wish to express my thanks to all members of the TM family and the Perth based KP group with whom I have interacted in recent times and sincerely acknowledge their input.

I wish to thank Manoj Kaul (Texas, US), Rakesh Safaya (Uttarkashi, India) and Sanjay Kaul (Boston, US) for their inspiration and encouragement.

This book would not have been possible without Vitasta Publishing. My sincere thanks and gratitude to my publisher Renu Kaul Verma, Managing Director of Vitasta, for making this book a reality and her suggestions, and Papri Sri Raman, my editor for her critical comments, useful suggestions and the great job that she has done with this book.

The original size of this manuscript was around 153,000 words. When I was writing the original manuscript, I was writing about my past life, which contained many things beyond Kashmir. My emotions got the better of me and perhaps I lost my focus in the process. The final manuscript came down to about 70,000 words, with focus on Kashmir alone, thanks to Papri's merciless red pen. I am grateful that you have brought the manuscript back on the rails to serve its intended purpose. Thank you, Papri. The remaining 70,000 words can be used in the future in another book, titled, *A Kashmiri Pandit in Exile*.

Lastly, I wish to thank my family for inspiration and encouragement for bearing with me through our life journey together and more recently through the writing phase of this book; for being patient enough to listen to me on a daily basis. My special thanks to my beautiful daughter, Deeksha Ladakhi Koul, for providing critical comments and useful suggestions from time to time.

# The Son Comes Home

*Every moment a breath of life is spent,*
*If I consider, not much of it remains.*
*O thou, whose fifty years have elapsed in sleep,*
*Wilt thou perhaps overtake them in these five days?*
*Shame on him who has gone and done no work.*
*The drum of departure was beaten but he has not*
*made his load.*
—Sa'di, 1210-1292
Gulistan

*If you greet a person and the person responds in kind,*
*That person considers you as equal in communication.*
—Bill K Koul

## Recalling 1989 Srinagar

A year of turmoil!

It was that time of the decade when Kashmir was definitely changing. Unfortunately, for the worse—from Sufism to Wahhabism to militancy. General life was not the same as before.

Violent militant activities—bomb blasts at prominent public places, targeted killings and encounters with the security forces were becoming regular features in Srinagar city and the surrounding major towns of Kashmir; as were frequent calls for *bandh* (civil strike) given by numerous militant and separatist organisations. Not many weeks passed by without one thing or the other.

Uncertainty was the new order of the day.

On the surface, life seemed to crawl and function, but not without hiccups and disruptions. One could not be sure if the next hour would be as normal or violent as the hour before. It was not unusual to see office-goers and students returning to their homes well before their scheduled times. The number of working days in a week reduced significantly.

It was not easy to differentiate between the so-called political leaders from the militant leaders; they all seemed to be working hand-in-glove with one another to confuse the situation and achieve their objectives. Chinese whispers abounded in the valley, mainly about large contingents of well-trained foreign mercenaries, from Pakistan, Afghanistan and other Islamic countries having sneaked into the valley to fight jihad against the infidels. Accordingly, Kashmiris of the majority Muslim community appeared to be excited about something that only they seemed to know about. Their body language had definitely changed. Some would openly make fun of members of the minority Pandit community. Their taunts and condescending remarks sounded ominous. It is also true, some Muslims provided subtle warnings to their Pandits friends, advising them to be careful and leave the valley for their safety.

On the horizon, a storm was surely building up, or so it seemed to Billu. However, an overwhelming majority of the Pandit community seemed to be oblivious to it. They appeared to adapt to the new life order as best as they could, similar to what they had done in the past for thousands of years. Either they were too thick skinned or too sanguine or just stupid. Many believed it was a temporary phase, as had been on numerous occasions in their recent past, and hoped the situation would return to 'normal' sooner than later.

Gifted by nature, Billu could see much beyond the eyes could see and the ears could hear. Like birds and other animals, he could clearly decipher the changing pattern in the air. Some would call this foresight but it was his sixth sense that warned him about an impending major turmoil and massive bloodshed in the valley. Every whisper over the radio wave and militant activity on ground zero, as reported in the print media or the television, petrified him.

Gradually over many long winter months, Billu became emotionally paralysed and too scared to leave his home for work or any social activity. Although he did not have any known personal enemies, who could have targeted him in the guise of being a part of the seething undercurrent that could be felt or heard more than seen, Billu did not rule out becoming a collateral casualty while travelling or walking through any street in the city where he had grown up. It was a peculiar psychological turnaround. The city was his playground, where he had learnt to walk, run, play football, scream in joy, cry with the crowd. He knew his fear was irrational. But fear it was. He was AFRAID.

Yet, he could not specify exactly what he was afraid of.

Fear was in the air. He could sense it, feel it though not define it. His intelligence told him to think it out, his instinct told him to run. His time at his place of work, REC Srinagar, where he was a Lecturer in Civil Engineering, dwindled with each week. A sudden change in the body language of his Muslim friends and colleagues was a barometer of something imminent. The smiles on their faces were fake and their handshakes were loose and less warm. They looked withdrawn from their non-Muslim colleagues. They knew something, which he did not. But he did sense something was wrong, actually very wrong.

Over time, he lost his self-confidence completely and suffered from an anxiety disorder. He saw his family doctor. Despite medication, he could neither sleep well nor eat well. Food was always tasteless and the sun burnt his eyes. His heart beat was always more than 100 per minute even when resting.

It appeared that the then Indian government, and the Indian security and intelligence agencies were caught napping and completely baffled by the well-planned politico-religious uprising in the valley to such an extent that he felt that the law and order was too weak to protect him and the members of his minority Pandit community. Very often, security personnel were caught defending themselves.

Billu started proactively warning everyone he met, but many of his Pandit friends and relatives thought he was going crazy. Despite that, he continued to make noises about the imminent turmoil on the horizon. He could not help but feel the storm brewing within him.

When he could take it no more, Billu decided to leave the valley permanently. Prior to leaving, he warned his parents that they too would have to leave the valley soon but, like all other learned elders of his community, they dismissed him, thinking he was timid and mad.

As it turned out, it had not been a sheer coincidence that about three years ago, during his very first arranged meeting with his future wife, Rekha, the possible exodus of the Pandit community from the valley was the only topic that they had discussed. During that meeting, he had tested her awareness about the religious and political situations in the valley, and she had passed that test. He was, thus, proved to be years ahead of his community, which claimed to be educated, intelligent and politically well informed.

In the second half of 1989, many prominent people from his Pandit community were killed by Muslim militants. The scare campaign had well and truly been unleashed. Finally, on 23 December 1989, accompanied by his wife and their two-year-old son, Billu left his beloved Kashmir.

On that day, he took a vow never to return to the land of his birth. He felt betrayed by his fellow Kashmiris and completely let down by the then governments—both state and the Central.

Billu was not mad. He was the only one who was not mad. As the world eventually saw, the storm that Billu had foreseen more than three years ago, did finally arrive about a month after his departure from the valley, on 19 January 1990, which displaced nearly half a million Pandits from the valley permanently and put to death thousands of Kashmiris—Pandits—killed by Muslim militants who fought their so-called jihad against 'infidels' and the security forces.

It has always baffled Billu as to why his elders could not see the trouble beforehand and brace themselves in time. Were they too intelligent? Had they lost their natural instincts and touch with nature? Was common sense so uncommon? Did their over-reliance on the five senses kill their sixth sense? Or was it simply a case of intelligent and educated people burying their head in sand, like the ostriches? Billu knows these questions may never be answered!

## 29 April 2012
**Faridabad, Haryana**

Twenty-two years on.

It was a warm sunny morning.

Billu was on a very short, five-day, visit to India, as a result of the sudden demise of Bhaisahib, his spiritual teacher, who had passed away eleven days ago. He had flown in from Perth (Australia) on 27 April to attend the 10$^{th}$ Day *Kriya*. He was scheduled to return to Perth two days later. Boba, his father, had also flown in from Jammu to attend the ritual and was also staying with Auntie, his father's sister.

Billu was quite melancholic that morning. His mood was pensive and deeply sombre, with grief written all over his face. He had just lost his spiritual father. All his conversations with Bhaisahib constantly floated through his mind. Bhaisahib had given him a new lease of life when he had initiated him into TM about twentyone years ago, in Jammu, in late 1991. It was a time when Billu was battling deep seated psychological pain and shock as a result of getting uprooted from his homeland. His sudden departure from Srinagar had preceded a tragic mass exodus of his community from Kashmir in January 1990. Daily meditation and spiritual guidance from Bhaisahib had helped him to make a relatively fast recovery. Regular meditation had not only strengthened his mind, it had also provided the much-needed clarity in his thoughts and a new resolve to live a meaningful life. In short, TM had proved to be a panacea.

Living in Australia, Billu had been regularly calling Bhaisahib, especially on Thursdays (also called the *Guru's Day*). He had last chatted with Bhaisahib on Monday, 16 April. The conversation had been fairly casual, although every time when they would chat, Billu would emerge enlightened. Such was the magic in Bhaisahib's simple and straight thought and his words. Even ordinary and simple words would carry a deep meaning and some learning for the other person. It all depended on the other person's interpretation, level of introspection and contemplation. Two days later, on 18 April, Bhaisahib had suddenly passed away. Billu did not come to know about it on that day. He called Bhaisahib's mobile phone, as usual, on the next Thursday but no one answered the phone. Billu thought perhaps Bhaisahib had been meditating at that time and had therefore not answered his call. On 20 April a fellow meditator had called from Delhi to inform Billu of Guruji's demise. Billu was shocked. By then, it was too late to attend the funeral; Bhaisahib's mortal remains had already been cremated. So he decided to attend his 10th Day *Kriya*.

As Billu was silently thinking about Bhaisahib on that sad morning, he received a telephone call from Srinagar from his uncle, Abujan. He was Billu's eldest aunt's husband.

In a soft but reassuring voice, Abujan enquired about Bhaisahib's family and conveyed his condolences. During the course of the conversation, Billu broke down and Abujan tried his best to console him.

About his own health, Abujan said that his recovery from a prostate surgery he had undergone about three months ago, had been very slow. As such, he still experienced a considerable degree of discomfort and a very disturbed sleeping pattern.

Bhaisahib's sudden departure had taken a heavy toll on Billu's psyche. He suffered from some degree of emotional insecurity due to uncertainness in life caused by the certainty of death. He had taken a considerable period of time to overcome the tragic loss of his friend Ashok Kaul (32) in 1989, and then of his brother-in-law Dr M L Pandit (45), in 2000. In more recent times, he had lost his mother-in-law in 2003, followed by his mother Rani (63) in 2008 and then his sister-in-law Bhavana (43) in 2010. Life seemed to be so unreliable and unfaithful, and death such a certainty. In that state of mind, Billu felt very concerned about Abujan's health and wanted to see him.

For the next ten minutes or so, his mind battled like a seesaw between his vow and a strong desire to meet Abujan.

The real problem was that it required him to fly to Srinagar, which required him to cross several mental hurdles. About 22 years ago, when he had departed from Srinagar, he had vowed that he would never return to the valley. Therefore, to meet Abujan, he would have to break his vow. Could he do it or did he want to do it? Those were the questions he had to answer.

Seeing his mental struggle, Boba offered to accompany him if he firmed up his decision to go. It was the monthly Ashtami day, dedicated to the Mother Goddess. Like many Kashmiri Pandits, Boba was also on fast on that day. Auntie was busy in the kitchen, preparing a special (*satvik*) meal for him, which Pandits generally consume during their fasts. Despite fasting, Boba sounded more than willing to accompany him to Srinagar. His cousin, Sameer Bradoo, offered to help them with the flight bookings. Within the next five minutes, Sameer said that some seats were available on a possible flight to Srinagar and he could book two tickets. Billu had to quickly make up his mind.

The next ten minutes saw Billu struggling and not able to decide. It was a warlike situation in his mind. To go or not to go! But he really wanted to see his ailing uncle. All eyes were focussed on him. Two hours earlier no one had envisaged this scenario. He had never discussed the possibility of this trip to Kashmir with his family in Perth. What would Rekha think? If something untoward happened to him during the trip, what would happen to his family? Was he going to compromise their future by putting himself in harm's way?

The stressful memories of his last day in Kashmir, 22 years ago, suddenly came alive. He tensed and felt a stitch in his gut. His heart beat faster, perhaps due to nervousness and gastritis, which was not much dissimilar to what he constantly experienced in 1989. Why was he doing all this? Was his life not important? Was he writing his own death sentence? All these turbulent questions flooded his mind. But, what if Abujan never recovered, God forbid!

Did Billu just need a real good reason to break his vow?

Perhaps, he had one at last. But was he willing to break his vow? Perhaps yes! He had been mentally ready for a while now. He had been away for two decades. The sharp edges of fear had blunted.

Was his vow higher than his concern for his uncle? No, absolutely not! His care for Abujan overcame his vow and all negative thoughts associated with his personal security and the general risk associated with the trip. As the positive emotions filled his mind, he told Boba that he was ready to fly to Srinagar and see Abujan. This was 2012. Not 1989.

The pressure suddenly shifted to Sameer. He had just witnessed a historical moment in Billu's life. But now he had to assist and somehow book those two air tickets. As luck would have it, Sameer managed to purchase the last two tickets on the last flight of the day to Srinagar. It was around 10 am and the flight was due to take off around 1.30 pm, so not much time was left. Billu and Boba packed their personal travel handbags in a jiffy. Around 11 am, Sameer drove them to the airport.

En route to the airport, Billu remained very quiet. He was still in an extreme emotional flux, with a barrage of differing thoughts flooding his mind. He was anxious to reach the airport before the check-in time, which can be a serious challenge if one gets caught up in a typical Delhi traffic jam. He also suffered from a strong sense of guilt towards his Perth-based family, especially because he had never ever discussed the possibility of a return visit to Srinagar with Rekha. Suddenly, he also felt a little uncomfortable on realising that he may have potentially placed himself in harm's way as if an invisible external force carried him to Srinagar. At the same time, he felt excited about meeting Abujan and his family. Given that he had never conceived return visit during the past 22 years, he also experienced a rare excitement of actually being in Srinagar once again and a real prospect of visiting Mata Ksheer Bhawani's shrine at Tulmul after a gap of more than twenty-two years.

Fortunately, the Delhi traffic was not very bad on that day. They reached the airport just in time. Billu believed someone was watching over him on that day! The security check did not take very long. As a result, they were left with about half an hour before boarding started, during which he called Rekha and surprised her with the news. As his return flight to Perth was scheduled two days later, she sounded confused and a little anxious. 'Why, what happened, is everyone alright?', she asked.

He tried to explain to her why and how he had suddenly decided to travel to Srinagar but she did not sound very reassured!

Albeit reluctantly, he also called Behanji, his aunt, to inform her that he was waiting to board a plane for Srinagar, thereby completely doing away with the surprise element associated with his visit. For a moment, she did not believe him, as she had given up on any possibility of his return to Srinagar. Only after she spoke with Boba, was she convinced.

Aboard the flight, Billu suddenly felt as if he was trapped. Before boarding the plane, he knew that he had the freedom to abort his trip and return to Auntie's home, which he could no longer do now. His nervousness was doused in the roaring sound of the engines. The flight cruised smoothly and his thoughts were relatively stable. However, as the plane approached for landing, the earlier sickening feelings returned. He forced himself to think about all the right reasons why he was in that situation. The bird's eye view of the valley, especially the picturesque snow-clad Peer Panchal peaks within the Himalayan ranges in the distance, provided a healthy diversion.

With his mind once again a battle ground, the plane touched down at Srinagar at about 2.45 pm. As the big bird rolled down the runway, his mind became numb. He gazed outside his seat window. The scene outside was very familiar. It appeared to be a cloudy and wet day. The tall poplar trees standing in the distance along the airport boundary and the green grass patches within the airport premises were reminiscent of the spring season. He remembered, with painful nostalgia, when he had travelled with his mother about eleven years ago from Delhi to Jammu, his plane had landed first at the Srinagar airport. On that day, after pleading desperately, the flight crew had allowed him to briefly disembark under very watchful and nervous eyes of the security personnel. He had stood on the tarmac for less than a minute and touched the ground in reverence to his homeland while taking a number of quick and deep breaths of the Srinagar air. On that day also, the sky was grey and not much different from this day, except that it had not rained on that day. He badly missed his mother.

When the plane stopped, he stood up robotically, like all other passengers, removed his hand bag from the overhead compartment and made a bee line towards the exit. He was acutely aware that he had returned home after a long twenty-two year period!

As soon as he stepped outside the plane, he took a deep gasp of the fresh Srinagar air and filled his lungs to capacity. After quickly descending the stairs, he bent down and touched the ground, as a repeat of the last gesture done eleven years ago.

With Boba walking by his side, he walked with purpose towards the arrival lounge with immense joy. Inside the terminal building, the settings and the human faces looked very familiar. For a moment, he thought as if he had never left the valley. Without any checked-in baggage, they did not take much time to exit the building and reach the carpark where Abujan's driver, Bashir, waited.

'Billu Bhaya, why haven't Bhabhiji and children come with you?' Bashir shouted from a distance, as soon as he saw them. They exchanged warm greetings and hugs and boarded Abujan's SUV. After leaving the airport premises, Billu saw numerous shops and houses which did not exist twenty-two years ago, lining both sides of the airport road. The Hyderpora Bypass Road crossing was unrecognisable. His earlier family house in nearby Rawalpora was not very far from that crossing. He felt nostalgic.

The road through Hyderpora and Bagaat, and the houses on either side, looked so familiar. The road seemed to be narrower than before, perhaps due to the higher number of road users, both pedestrians and the mixed traffic. The muddy kerbs reminded him of the past and how difficult it used to be for pedestrians to walk along the road during and after rains.

The Ram Bag Bridge and the surrounding structures across the bridge looked in a dilapidated condition; with piles of rubble and some construction equipment idling along the road. Jehangir Hotel chowk looked busier than before, with a flyover through the chowk making it unrecognisable and congested. The crossing appeared to be less impressive than the last time he had seen it. The quality of construction of the overpass bridge looked inferior and shabby, with thicker than (international) standard concrete beams and rough finishes. New shops and huge bill boards were quite visible, loudly proclaiming that the locals had access to international branded items of daily use. However, on a more careful observation, the whole area appeared to have gone backwards in terms of the overall planning of the city and the quality and appearance of the infrastructure. Traffic looked more disorderly than before.

The SUV turned left towards Batmalloo. From a distance, the New Secretariat building looked far less appealing and run down than before. The Batmalloo area was totally unrecognisable. Thereafter, traffic through the downtown area was considerably slow.

Numerous vegetable and fruit stalls and vendors squatting in front of the regular shops considerably narrowed down the trafficable width of the road. He wondered about the existence of the municipality and the relevant planning and enforcement authorities.

As the SUV passed through the Idgah area, childhood memories came alive. In his teenage years, before the family had shifted to Rawalpora, he had played lots of cricket in the Idgah grounds during several winter breaks. His Budhgair (in Alikadal) cricket team had comprised closely knit members of both Muslim and Pandit communities, in roughly equal numbers. Their cricket team had won and lost numerous matches in those fearless and fun-filled years. He missed his childhood cricket mates and wondered where were they now; how they looked now and would he be able to recognise them? Time would have definitely changed everyone's appearance.

The road and the area in front of the main gate of Sher-e-Kashmir Institute of Medical Sciences, at Soura, looked crowded with haphazard traffic and people everywhere. The pattern of pedestrian and vehicular movement indicated continued absence of planning on part of people at the helm. It seemed public transport vehicles could stop anywhere to pick up and drop off passengers, which did not appear to be much different than before. However, due to a significantly higher density of the mixed traffic, the public and trafficable areas looked much more crowded than before. Due to the rain, the roads were wet, with numerous potholes and muddy conditions, which looked quite familiar. Not much seemed to have changed during all these years.

After crossing Soura, the area looked rather unfamiliar and Billu asked Bashir about the route that he was taking.

'Ninety Feet Road, which has been constructed by Abujan. It extends from Soura to Panduchh and has greatly eased the traffic in this area', Bashir replied proudly. Suddenly, Bill remembered Abujan's other contributions in the development of local infrastructure.

Finally, after driving slowly through several narrow lanes that link the Ninety-Feet Road with the original Ganderbal Road, the SUV reached Behanji's house at Ahmad Nagar (Umarheer), located on the banks of Aanchar Lake, between Buchhpora and Gandherbal. It was about 4 pm by that time.

Behanji's domestic helper, Rashid, was waiting outside the gate. As soon as he saw the SUV, he opened the gate, with excitement clearly visible on his young face. Inside, the traditional ceremonial white lime powder drawings were visible on both sides of the long driveway. At the far end of the driveway, a large white banner printed with colourful flowers and a WELCOME sign had been fixed to a telephone pole on one end and a poplar tree on the other end. All these efforts loudly beamed the excitement and sentiments of the hosts.

After the SUV stopped on a gravel driveway closer to the house, they were warmly received and hugged by the waiting hosts. Behanji, Abujan, Billu's cousin Manju and several domestic helpers all looked excited. Billu was then led towards a ceremonial *vyuug* and made to stand at its centre, in line with the Kashmiri traditions for welcoming an important guest. A *vyuug* is circular in shape, about 1 m in diameter, and made with saw dust of different colours. It usually takes up to an hour or so to decorate it. Once completed, it looks like a beautiful floor painting.

Within about 15 minutes of entering the house, Billu announced his intention to visit Mata Ksheer Bhawani's shrine at Tulmul before he could allow himself to settle down. Although Behanji and Abujan strongly insisted that they should first have a cup of tea to freshen up, Boba announced that he was on the Ashtami fast and would break his fast only at Tulmul. Respecting his sentiments, Abujan asked Bashir to immediately drive them to Tulmul. A light drizzle had just started again.

On way to Tulmul, vast paddy fields, lined by poplar trees and mountains, some clad with a fresh snowfall, brought back memories of his distant past.

Billu realised that he was actually in Kashmir and it was not a dream. To Boba's discomfort, he rolled down his car window and allowed the cold fresh air to come in and fill his lungs. It was a magical feeling; he was not only physically at home, he was actually breathing its air. For a few moments, he was again filled with nostalgic memories of his past. After crossing Ganderbal, beautiful people walking along the road through the Tulmul village distracted him. He felt very much at home in familiar surroundings; everything seemed to make sense.

Tulmul is located about 7 to 8 km from Behanji's house. It took them about 20 minutes to reach there. After disembarking from the SUV, he stood motionless for a few moments, looking towards the main entrance of the shrine. The drizzle had completely stopped. The view of the security personnel at the entrance and the presence of barricades (sand bags and barbed wire) in front of the main entrance made him sick and deeply sad. After taking a deep breath, he looked up, with misty eyes. Oh my Mother, do you also need security?

The clouds in the sky looked patchy, with different shades of grey clouds and isolated patches of blue sky in between.

After going through the security check, they walked along the middle of the main driveway towards the inner shrine complex. It was a very humbling experience. During his childhood days, he used to play with the other kids in those park sections and gazebos that flanked both sides of the driveway. On the occasion of *Jaysht Ashtami* (usually in the month of

June, celebrated as the birthday of the Mother Goddess), he remembered how numerous hawkers and vendors would squat on both sides on the driveway and sell ice creams, candies, toys and so many household items. It used to be so much fun in those good old days. Most of his Tulmul memories were associated with his grandmother, Amaji, who used to stay there for a few days at a time, particularly during summer, around Jaysht Ashtami. Billu had always accompanied her.

On reaching the main gate of the inner shrine complex, they rang the ceremonial bell, which sounded so divine and peaceful, just like the old days.

Before entering the fenced shrine complex, one has to remove one's shoes, take a bath or wash hands, feet and face as a minimum. Over the past two decades, the whole infrastructure around the fenced complex appeared to have significantly improved. The area looked much cleaner and organised, with much better facilities, under the care of the Indian Army.

A number of grocery and food shops, which also sell the *puja* items and the *dharamshala* buildings (pilgrim quarters) in the background comprised a new development around the fenced area. The stream flowing outside in the front of the complex looked much cleaner, with proper concrete steps on both its banks from where one could enter the water for a dip, or wash face and hands etc. The pre-cast paving blocks looked very clean and in a good condition.

Twenty-two years ago, the Koul family were regular customers of Pandit Vaish Nath, who would provide them with a mat for sitting inside the fenced complex, the puja items and cooked food. His shop and all other older shops were nowhere to be seen now. Boba went to Ramji Halwai's shop to procure the necessary puja items and introduced Billu to him. The meeting reminded Billu of a significant change in the era, from Vaish Nath to Ramji. The feeling was quite mixed, mainly because it was nothing like in the past. This was an entirely different scene, with a different setting and new actors playing their part. After completing the initial greetings etc. they entered the fenced shrine complex, with a *thali* (a large steel plate) that held the necessary puja items in Boba's hand.

The puja was performed under a covered area, in front of the main temple, by a resident Kashmiri priest. Billu missed Rani very much. While reciting the *shalokas* in praise of the Mother Goddess, he felt the constant presence of his mother around him and remembered her voice when she would pray. Boba, as usual, was fully absorbed in his prayers with full dedication; he paid an undivided attention to the puja ceremony. With tears flowing continuously down his cheek, Billu prayed for Bhaisahib's peace, as well as for Abujan's good health. He also missed his family back home in Perth and prayed for them.

As is customary, after completing the puja, the worshippers walk around the main temple a number of times, praying all the time. Some once, some three times, some eleven times, some 101 times and so on. They also went round the temple several times, praying all along. During those rounds, Billu missed his grandfather, Tathaji a lot too. He remembered the spot where Tathaji would sit and recite the entire *Panchastavi* (a sacred book with five chapters of praises for the Mother Goddess) in a sweet voice, with his body rocking from side to side and tears flowing continuously down his cheek. For the interest of the reader, it is important to highlight that Tathaji was not a regular temple goer. He would not usually visit the shrine on a public holiday. On the contrary, a few times in the year, he would take a day off from his school and visit the shrine. On numerous such occasions, Billu had accompanied him and witnessed firsthand Tathaji's utmost faith, love and dedication to the Mother. In Billu's mind, therefore, Tathaji was more of a spiritual person, rather than a religious one. His spirituality was a very personal and private affair for him. He did not believe in showing off his religious beliefs. Very few people knew about this aspect of Tathaji's life.

It was already past 5.45 pm when they returned to Ramji Halwai's shop again. Boba broke his Ashtami fast with a cup of *kahwa* and some *puris* (made of water chestnut flour) at the shop. Some *halwa* (semolina pudding), *luchi* (deep-fried flat bread) and *nadroo monjas* (lotus root, fried in rice flour batter) were quickly packed for the host family.

Around 6.30 pm, they were back at Abujan's home and were seated comfortably on a Kashmiri *gabba* (a woollen embroidered carpet) in the *hamam* area (a warm room, usually adjacent to the kitchen). A *dastarkhan* (a dinner sheet) was soon laid on the carpeted floor. According to Kashmiri traditions, as it was evening, *sheer chai*, also known as *noon chai* (salted tea) was served with all the niceties that they had just brought from Tulmul, along with fresh *kulcha* (crisp scones) and *talewor* (bagels with sesame seed) from a local baker. Boba ate only some freshly cut fruit, being on a fast.

Over tea, the conversations mainly revolved around Abujan's health and Bhaisahib's sudden demise. They also talked about life in Perth; heat in Delhi; security and general life in Kashmir and the current state of infrastructure in Srinagar city and the surrounding areas. Around 7 pm, there was a power outage; it was the turn of the local area to go without power for a couple of hours that day of the week. That reminded Billu of the power cuts in his past life in Srinagar. Obviously, the power supply had not improved much in the last twenty-two years. Rashid rushed in with a gas-lamp to light the room.

Although it was nearly the end of May, *kangris* (fire pot) were still being used in the house. For travelling purposes, Billu had brought just one sweater from Perth for keeping him warm in the planes, which he was wearing. But that sweater was not enough to keep warm on that evening, especially after such a hectic day. He felt cold and asked for a kangri, then wrapped himself with a *dusa* (a thin woollen blanket). It was such a nice and cosy feeling, just like the good old days! The cosy feeling also brought back terrifying memories of his previous life in Srinagar, which were exacerbated by the dark nooks and corners in the room and the people silhouetted against the light of the lamp.

Suddenly he became acutely conscious of being physically 12,000 km away from his family. He also woke up to the fact that he was in the same Kashmir where he had felt extremely stressed, depressed and anxious due to fear twenty-two years ago and wondered what would happen to his family if something untoward happened to him. Similar thoughts had gripped his mind in the morning at Delhi; but now they had returned with greater vengeance.

He felt extremely claustrophobic and started panicking. His heartbeat became noticeably faster. The memory of 1989 made him belch in fear. His forehead and hands were moist with perspiration. Impulsively, he shed the dusa. Fortunately, due to poor light in the room, no one noticed his anxiety and nervousness.

Realising that he did not have any avenue of escape from the situation, he asked for a glass of cold water. That helped. He also purposefully engaged in more meaningful conversations with Abujan and the other members of the family. He learnt Abujan had not been sleeping during nights due to considerable discomfort after his surgery and also because of his lifelong habit of offering *namaz* twice every night.

Around 9.30 pm, the power supply was restored and the room was bright again. Dinner was announced and a dastarkhan was laid on the floor in the centre of the room. A number of bowls containing vegetarian dishes were placed on it. Billu noticed all these dishes were among his favourites. He felt instantly hungry. Laying a dastarkahn is an elaborate task and takes a few minutes before all necessary crockery and cutlery are placed over it in an organised manner. He had to wait before he could start eating, but not for very long. The food was tasty. Boba had only some freshly cut fruit and a small bowl of yogurt. Over dinner, the chitchat continued and he felt relatively more comfortable than before. The small talk continued over a tasty desert. 11 pm, and it was time to go to bed.

Behanji and Abujan accompanied Boba and Billu to their upstairs bedroom, which overlooked the Anchaar Lake. After getting familiarised with the bedroom, the hosts left wishing their guests good night. After Boba entered his bed, Billu switched the light off and entered his own bed. Sudden darkness in the room made him feel a little uncomfortable. He got out of his bed and drew a couple of curtains wide open to allow the nightlight to fill the room. He felt a little better and walked back to his bed. While trying to sleep, he prayed and hoped the night would be as safe as the day before. With his physical and mental fatigue, he did not take very long to fall asleep.

He woke up the next morning in wonder that he had been absolutely safe during the night and, therefore, felt more assured about his safety. Obviously, he had unnecessarily created a little storm in his mind on the previous evening, as a result of his past memories.

This day, 30 April 2012, was a brand new day. It promised a new start to his life in so far as his identity as a Kashmiri was concerned. He also promised himself that he would put his past behind and move on, which was necessary for him to spend the remaining valuable time in Kashmir with relative ease and with a more relaxed mindset, with the hosts, particularly with Abujan for whom he was actually there. His return flight to Delhi was scheduled around noon the next day and he was scheduled to fly back to Perth the same evening.

Breakfast was served around 8.30 am. Being a vegetarian, Billu had Kashmiri *kahwa* (green tea) with *paneer pakora* (fried ricotta cheese chunks in chickpea flour) and buttered *girda* (baker's flat bread). Other members of the family had omelette, stuffed with finely chopped vegetables.

Around 10.30 am, the sun shone brightly for a change and everyone moved out to the front lawn of the house to soak up some sunshine and indulge in gossip over another round of tea. For a change, this time it was regular Lipton's tea, with biscuits. The morning newspaper frequently changed hands. After a while, Behanji asked Billu if he would like to visit any particular place in Srinagar and he said, no. She said he should at least take a quick tour of the city, but he showed no interest. He reiterated that he wanted to spend as much time as possible with Abujan, that being the basic purpose of his visit. He also clarified that he was not a tourist and, therefore, had no interest in any sightseeing. However, Behanji persisted and Billu had to give in but only on the condition that Abujan would come along as well. It was also decided that it would be a short three-hour round trip via the new Foreshore Road along Dal Lake and touch Hazratbal, Nishat Bagh and Harwan.

They started around 11.30 am from Ahmad Nagar. As the SUV reached Hazratbal, Billu requested Bashir to turn towards the Dargah, at Hazratbal. He wanted to pay his respects there. Historically, first as a student and then as a teacher, he had spent nearly eleven years at the Regional Engineering College (REC), Srinagar; the campus is located adjacent to the Dargah. Furthermore, by his own admission, way back in 1978, at the time of his admission to the REC, Boba had secretly entrusted his welfare and safety to the *Dargah*. It was no surprise that, before leaving Kashmir in December 1989, Billu and Rekha had visited and offered respects at the Dargah for fourteen consecutive days in late November/early December 1989. So, it was only appropriate that he visit the Shrine and pay his respects there to mark his homecoming.

On alighting from the SUV at the *Dargah*, he was overwhelmed. With misty eyes, he walked towards the entrance of the Dargah premises, hands joined together, in complete reverence. His faith had not depleted through all these years. On reaching the main entrance of the Dargah, he kneeled to mark his respect and then stood up, still and quiet, with eyes closed and hands held together. After a few minutes, he turned around, left the entrance gate and boarded the waiting SUV, without saying anything to anyone.

After leaving the Shrine, the SUV took the Foreshore Road, which had been constructed during his absence from Kashmir, along the periphery of the world famous Dal Lake.

The view of Dal Lake and the Shankaracharya Hill in the background was as picturesque as it always had been, although the lake showed numerous patches of weed. It did not take very long for them to reach the famous Nishat Bagh. By then, the weather conditions had changed and it had started raining. The dark rain clouds along the Zabrawan hills that envelope the garden on the east, hung very low and hid nearly the upper half of the hills. The view of the majestic terraced garden at the foothills of Zabarwan, with partly clouded hills in the background, was a very captivating view as the clouds moved aside for a few minutes and allowed the sun to peep through, bathing the garden in bright sunshine. The umbrellas were folded and they ate hot popcorns.

After bidding farewell to Nishat Garden, they moved towards Harwan, another garden at the downstream side of the Sarband Dam. Sarband is a rainwater reservoir located in the picturesque foothills of Zabarwan hills and serves as one of the main sources of drinking water catering to the Srinagar city. They spent about half an hour in admiring the natural beauty of the place and then left.

They reached home around 2.30 pm. Lunch was served in the warm hamaam room. His favourite vegetarian cuisine was served. The family spent the afternoon talking. Soon the day was at an end and tea was served.

Time seemed to fly very fast on this day. Due to the mountains, the sun sets much earlier in Srinagar than the plains of India and the days are relatively much shorter. Due to a dark rain cloud cover, it was already dark by about 6.30 pm. This evening appeared to bring contrasting feelings than the evening before. He felt much more relaxed and at home. He did not perspire, nor did he feel anxious. On the contrary, he realised that his visit had been a little too short and he ought to have stayed for a few days more. But at this stage, he could not extend his stay. Once again, he reminded himself to maximise his interaction with the hosts. After dinner he returned to the bedroom. He suddenly started missing Kashmir.

Next day, the sun was out quite early in the morning. After breakfast, the next couple of hours were spent in recapitulating all that was said in the last two days. Billu was made to promise to return to Srinagar along with his family.

At about around 11 am, Behan ji, Abujan and all members of the household reached the outer gate of the house to bid Billu and his father good bye. It was time to leave.

After hugs, kisses and tears, the SUV left for the airport. Billu could not control his tears on the way. His emotions were akin to those of a person leaving his parents behind and going away on a long trip. However, on reaching the airport premises, he was forced to return to reality. The multi-tiered security before entering the Srinagar airport premises and on reaching the airport terminal, requires a passenger to be physically and mentally fit to undergo the rigours of an elaborate security drill. In the present day and age, there is no place for emotions while you go through the general formalities at an airport, in particular, the Srinagar airport. While waiting in the departure lounge, he missed Behanji and Abujan. But, once the boarding started, he prepared himself mentally for the hot weather ahead in Delhi and then his onward journey to Perth in the evening.

Aboard the plane, he promised himself to return the next year, which he did, now that he was reconnected with his home.

**Home Sweet Home**
Billu visited Kashmir every summer since his first 2012 return visit. Each visit was over a maximum period of one week. Unlike his previous visits in 2013 to 2015, which were peaceful and uneventful, his recent 6-day visit to Kashmir in early July 2016 was stressful and reminiscent of the stressful and unsettled 1989-1990 period.

On the night of his first day in Srinagar in July 2016, the valley was hit by a massive rainstorm, which caused widespread damage to numerous trees and lighter structures. On the evening of 8 July, the news of killing of a young militant leader by the security forces spread like wildfire and brewed tension in the air.

On 9 July 2016, Billu witnessed repeated invasion of a nearby CRPF camp over the course of the day by several mobs of stone-pelting youth (generally 10 to 25 years old), who shouted vicious abuses at the security forces, provoking them to come out of their camp. The CRPF jawans exercised utmost restraint and no one was injured on that day. It seemed the youth were acting outside the control of their families. A Muslim lady from across the road came out of her house and yelled at them to go back to their homes. They broke all her glass window panes. A person shouted, she is a *mukhbir* (an informer).

Billu managed to reach the airport by 8 am on the 10th morning, thanks to Bashir Ahmad (Abujan's driver), who took the initiative and dropped him off at the airport risking his own life. On way to the airport, Billu observed the carnage left on the roads by the protesters on the day before. In the airport, hundreds of other travellers camped in an open ground. The situation was warlike. Most of the tourists and pilgrims wanting to leave Srinagar had been camping there since about 3 am that morning. In the airport lounge, many travellers were heard swearing that they would never return to Kashmir. Many visitors reported that their hotels were invaded by angry mobs around 10 to 11 pm on the night before and they had feared for their lives.

On the plane were a couple who had come for the Amarnath Shrine yatra. However, on sensing trouble, they had aborted their plans. Billu felt ashamed for the state of affairs in his homeland.

## Abujan

Abujan has provided considerable moral and emotional support to the Koul family in their rainy days. Eight years ago, when Rani passed away, most of the relatives would come and go during the days of mourning. Abujan had come from Srinagar the moment he heard the news and stayed put for a couple of weeks, standing beside the grieving family like a rock. During that time and, thereafter, he provided constant emotional support to both Boba and Billu and, of course, to the other members of the extended family.

By his own standards, living at any relative's house was quite unusual and unheard of, considering that Abujan seldom left his home in Srinagar. During those days of utter grief, he was notably the one person from whom Billu derived the most of psychological and emotional support. With his intelligent humour and ready wit, he provided a significant distraction from grief.

Billu had looked up to him in his growing years, especially as a student engineer. His undergraduate thesis was based on 'water supply network in greater Srinagar', which was based on the information and technical data provided by Abujan. In the mid-eighties, he strongly advised Billu, after his graduation, to qualify for the IAS and serve as a civil servant. Abujan's effect had been so profound that Billu even acquired a standing posture and walking gait similar to Abujan. While standing and walking, Abujan would lean slightly forward, out of humility and modesty. He never stood proud. Billu saw him as an extremely noble and virtuous person, just like a fully laden fruit tree, unlike a poplar tree that stands proud.

Abujan is widely respected for his honesty and sincerity but also feared for his no-nonsense approach. Abujan led a relatively very simple but an upright life. Abujan's personal neat qualities, professionalism and honesty had always deeply impressed Billu. By his own standards, if there had to be an ideal family man that Billu had ever come across, it was Abujan. Except smoking cigarettes in his younger days, Abujan had no vices. He had personally tutored his children through their schooling days.

Between 1981 and 1986, when Abujan was a Superintending Engineer in the Water Works engineering department, Billu lived at his aunt's home. Initially as an undergrad student and, thereafter, as a teacher at REC, Billu's stay would range between a couple of days and a couple of months. Those days, Billu was amazed to see how Abujan spent his day. It was unlike any other person whom he had ever met.

He woke up around 4.00 am and offered morning *namaz* by 5. By 5.30 am he would go for a morning walk and get milk from a dairy farm. By 6.15 am he would begin cooking breakfast for the kids and pack their lunch for school. He would then help his young daughters get ready for school, comb the hair and help them with homework. At 7.00 am the kids' school lunches were packed and Abujan served breakfast to all the kids and Billu.

By 8.00 am he was ready and left for work; Billu went with him and got a lift to college. Abujan returned home by 5.30 pm, again helped the children with their homework. The evening tea was served with Kashmiri baker's bread. Soon after, he offered *namaz*. His long day ended after 10 pm.

Sunday used to be the only weekend day for Abujan. During the first half of the Sunday, without fail, people from the adjoining areas would make a bee-line to Abujan's house and seek his advice to resolve their personal and domestic issues. He never seemed to get tired. When people greeted him at his home or on the road, he used to bow his head a little, lower his eyes and raise his right hand towards the sky, thus, personifying a truly noble and humble gentleman.

Sunday afternoon used to be relatively more relaxed, but he never wasted them in watching television or in any idle gossip. Instead, he would keep busy with reading engineering text books and tutoring of his children. His favourite topics of discussions included, and still continue to include, science and engineering, literature, morality and social ethics. He has not been observed to be indulging in any political and social gossip.

In his student years, Billu never saw Boba following such a life style. In contrast to Abujan, Boba would wake up around 8 am; leave for his work around 8.45 am and return home around 9 pm, sometimes past that time; eat dinner around 11 pm and go to bed around 12 midnight. There was absolutely no comparison between the two. For that matter, he has not been able to compare Abujan's high moral thinking and life style with any other person.

Abujan had been the main brainchild and a major driving force for the creation of the Jhelum Valley Medical College, which has provided medical education to numerous Kashmiri students. He also played a significant role in the construction of Dr Ali Jan Road, extending from Maulana Azad Bridge to Khanyaar, through downtown Srinagar.

Abujan has also been very active in social engineering and reforms. In the mid to late eighties, singlehandedly he got rid of a high profile prostitution centre, which was being run at that time in two houseboats on the banks of Nagin Lake. Although he had full support from the state government of the time, he still had to overcome and prevail upon a very strong and influential opposition that had been involved in running the racket. His single-minded and determined fight eventually took a big toll on his health and he had to be admitted to Sher-e-Kashmir Institute of Medical Sciences for a few weeks after suffering from severe mental and physical stress and exhaustion. After the racket was busted, he made sure the house boat owners were relocated and provided with alternative new housing at Bemina, Srinagar.

Abujan has been a seeker of knowledge. He is also a student of nature and likes to uncover her mysteries. He believes it is knowledge that makes a man's life healthier (morally, physically and mentally) and is worth pursuing. He is a strong supporter of girls' education.

Once Billu asked him, 'Abujan, what is your opinion about hijab for women?'

Abujan replied, '*Hijab is for both men and women, not only for women. Men should respect women and not stare at them while speaking with them or walking on the road.*'

More recently, Billu asked him about the status of women in Islam.

Abujan replied, 'Their status is equal and must be considered to be equal. On the basis of their physical appearances and anatomies, it seems God has provided men and women with different strength sets to perform their respective roles in life.

Together, they make a complete set. Both men and women have their respective strengths and weaknesses; ie. what a man can do easily, a woman may not be able to do with equal ease and efficiency and vice-versa. In the Holy Quran, there is a verse which tells men to provide physical protection to women because, by their natural constitution and build-up, women are relatively physically weaker than men. However, this verse has been widely misinterpreted by numerous religious teachers, who preach that a man can own a woman as he is superior, which is totally wrong.'

If only we had more men like Abujan in this world, the world would have been a much better place!

Abujan's father was Mufti Qawam-ud-din Farooqi, the then Mufti Azam of Kashmir. His elder brother, Mufti Bashir-ud-din Farooqi is the current Mufti Azam of Kashmir. The family hails originally from Iran.

On the advice of an astrologer, Abujan was given away by his biological parents soon after his birth. His foster mother, a distant aunt, adopted him. She was a poor childless widow. During his initial 10-15 years, till his foster mother's demise, Abujan lived a very hard life. In his own words, his foster mother loved him a lot. But she did not have enough food to provide. He remembers going to bed without eating dinner several days every month despite having his affluent biological parents living next doors. His foster mother never asked for any help from anyone. He deeply respected her self-respect and pride. He would help her around the house and fetch many pails of drinking water every day from a public tap near his home.

He returned to his biological parents after his foster mother died. Being a bright student, he completed his Bachelor's degree in Civil Engineering from Patna in the late fifties, followed by Master's degree in Public Health Engineering from Calcutta, about two decades later. He retired as Chief Engineer in Public Health Engineering. Being modest and full of humility, he has never claimed any credit for making any positive life changes in a considerable number of people. His humble nature seems to be a result of his early life experience with his foster mother.

# The Day of Exile

*We were expecting help from comrades.*
*What we were assuming was completely wrong.*
*Till the time when the tree of friendship might bear fruit,*
*We are off now, but we have sown a seed.*
*Bandying words is not the dervish style.*
*If it were, we have some old scores with you.*
*Your eye's sly look has the feint of war.*
*We make a mistake: we take it for peace.*
*The beauty of your rose bush was not of itself heart-enkindling:*
*We cast the spell of devotion over it.*
*Subtleties have passed, but no one complained:*
*We did not damage the dignity of respect.*
*He said, 'You yourself surrendered to the heart, O Ha'fiz:*
*We have not sent anyone the tax-gatherer.'*

—Hafez
*Divan of Hafez*, translated by Peter Avery

The day was 23 December 1989.

There are two types of people in this world, those who mostly live in the past and carry a whole load of the past baggage on their mind; and there are those who deliberately try to make a conscious effort in forgetting their painful past in order to forge ahead in their lives. Billu had tried his best to be the second type. Till his return visit to Srinagar 22 years later, he had tried to push his painful past below his conscious mind. But his return visit to his homeland brought everything up, everything that he remembered since his earliest days.

Tragic events leave permanent deep scars.

Since 1988, Billu had been struggling with extreme anxiety disorder, driven mainly by numerous violent incidents in Kashmir, which included violent public demonstrations, frequent shutdowns, random bomb blasts and targeted individual shootings. As a result, he had been feeling extremely insecure, within his house and outside. He had not been sleeping well during nights over the last several months.

His last night in Srinagar that cold December was no different. He had prayed for good weather to allow the resumption of flights to Srinagar from the plains of India. The flights had been suspended for the last two days due to bad weather conditions in the north of India. He was desperate to leave Kashmir.

He and his family were originally scheduled to take the 2.30 pm flight two days earlier on 21 December. However, due to a very heavy snowfall on that day, all flights to Srinagar were cancelled, much to his disappointment. The cancellation of his flight was announced on All India Radio that morning. The next day also, Srinagar had experienced a heavy snowfall, but the weather forecast for 23 December looked promising. As such, on the night of 22 December, he had decided to reach the airport very early in the morning to be able to manage three seats on any plane out of Srinagar.

Around 7 am on 23 December, he anxiously surveyed the sky outside his parents' bedroom windows to assess the weather conditions. To his delight, the sky looked clear. In anticipation of possible arrival of flights that day, he excitedly urged Rekha to get ready for the airport.

Boba's driver, Muhammed Shafi, arrived at about 8 am. Within a few minutes, Billu left for the airport with his young family. Boba accompanied them to the airport. As the sky had been clear during the last night, the atmospheric temperature had dipped to a sub-zero level. Piles of frozen dirty snow were visible on either side of the road to the airport. The journey took less than 20 minutes from their Rawalpora home. Half the battle was won, he thought. Billu promised himself that if he was not able to fly out that day, he would request the airport or the air force authorities to provide him and his family with temporary overnight shelter. He was determined not to return to Rawalpora in any case. He perceived an existential threat to his personal security and the security of his family or, for that matter, to any person in Kashmir.

He believed Kashmir was heading into an uncertain environment of commotion, volatility and bloodshed.

The airport security personnel allowed them to enter the terminal building on checking their earlier air tickets for 21 December.

Once inside the building, much to his anxiety, he discovered there were many other people like him whose flights had been cancelled over the past two days due to bad weather. The airline staff advised the passengers that once the incoming flights were confirmed, those passengers who had confirmed tickets for that day would be the first ones to receive boarding cards. Thereafter, the waitlisted passengers would be served on a first come first served basis.

Accordingly, the waitlisted passengers were asked to fall in a separate queue. Billu was fifth or sixth in his queue of waitlisted passengers. No flights were announced till almost mid-day. He was sick from anxiety due to possibility of not being able to leave that day if the flights did not arrive or if no seats were available for the waitlisted passengers. He kept chewing black pepper kernels. He checked his pulse. His heart beat was 180 to 200 times per minute. He gasped for safety and freedom.

In late October 1989, Billu visited Swami Vishud Chaitanya, who lived at downtown Bohri Kadal, to seek a cure for his anxiety by spiritual means. The Swamjii gave Billu a packet of black pepper kernels, mixed with *basm* (ashes) and told him to chew the pepper three times a day or whenever he felt overly nervous.

Those days, the Swamiji was a very famous person in the valley. It was common knowledge that several government ministers and top bureaucrats visited him on a regular basis. Billu had known Swamiji since late 1977, when he was about 15 years old. Those days, Swamji was a regular visitor at his aunt's home. Swamiji lived at a nearby temple with his assistant in downtown Maharaj Gunj. They both hailed from Tamil Nadu and possibly struggled with the cold weather of Kashmir and Billu's aunt offered them assistance in all possible ways. In that winter of 1977-78, after taking his Year 11 Board Examinations, Billu would also regularly visit his aunt's home to play cricket and badminton with his cousins.

Around that time, Swamiji had been undertaking some kind of research in palmistry and, by then, had read nearly 80,000 hands. Billu visited him at his temple residence, where Swamiji took a carbon print of his hand and made a number of predictions, including one about his PUC examinations marks. All his predictions subsequently came true. Swamji was also a student of science, he would subscribe to a monthly science magazine called *Science Digest*. Billu often borrowed the magazines. This led to a regular interaction between the two, which generally involved discussions on various science related topics. But, after Billu's parents moved to Rawalpora in 1981, the interactions between the two ceased completely. Within the next eight years, the Swami's fame as a spiritual guru had spread far and wide in Kashmir. One had to take a proper appointment to meet with him. This was the Swamiji who had given Billu an anxiety cure.

During the course of the day, Billu ran high on adrenaline. They had not eaten anything at the airport since their arrival. With his anxious state of mind, food was the last thing that he could think of. Around 1 pm, an announcement on the PA system said that a Srinagar bound plane had left Delhi, via Chandigarh, and the passengers should form a queue for checking-in. This caused a buzz amongst those who had confirmed tickets. After the confirmed ticketed passengers were checked in, the queue of the waitlisted passengers started moving. Billu prayed for luck! With each minute, his impatience and anxiety increased. His belching became too frequent and his heart raced faster out of sheer desperation.

As an anticlimax, around 2.30 pm, the ticketing window closed and he was very close to the window at that time. So near and yet so far!

Billu felt petrified and cursed his luck, with tears of desperation in his eyes. He approached the airline staff and requested for their special consideration. He was advised that the waitlisted passengers also had a good chance to travel if a scheduled (Airbus) flight from Bombay would take off for Srinagar. The airline personnel further explained that, as the Airbus plane had advanced night landing system, unlike a Boeing plane, it could land at the Srinagar airport even in darkness. This was great news. He thanked God; all was not lost yet. He prayed harder and promised that if he managed to reach Delhi that evening, he would first visit the Hanuman temple at Connaught Place. In Kashmir, in the pre-1990 era, since the Maharaja's days, butcher shops used to be generally closed on Tuesdays. Being an animal lover and vegetarian since his childhood, Billu had been a great devotee of Lord Hanuman.

As luck would have it, at around 4 pm, an announcement was made on the PA system that the Airbus flight from Bombay had taken off and was on its way to Srinagar. The waitlisted passengers were accordingly advised to queue up for ticketing purposes. This announcement sounded like a God-sent message, so sweet. He received confirmed tickets and boarding cards. After the security check, they settled in the departure lounge.

After some minutes, to his amazement, they were joined by some passengers who had been issued boarding cards for the earlier flight. Reportedly, that flight did not arrive as the pilot had refused to take off from Chandigarh due to bad weather conditions in the area. So, only those passengers from that flight, who had connecting flights from Delhi to other parts of the country, had been issued boarding cards for the Airbus flight. He realised how lucky he had been! If he would have succeeded in getting seats on the earlier (now cancelled) flight, he would have been stuck in Srinagar because he did not have any connecting flight from Delhi. He thanked God once again and realised that whatever happens; happens for one's own good!

The Airbus flight landed at the Srinagar airport at dusk in poor light. The plane took off after 5.30 pm and, with that, all his anxiety disappeared. His pulse returned to around 80 beats per minute and his belching reduced considerably. During the flight, he thanked God constantly for being able to leave Srinagar that day. He also started preparing himself mentally for Delhi. The plane landed at Delhi around 7 pm, under lights. This was his first experience of landing in artificial light conditions. They took a taxi and reached Auntie's house by about 8 pm. After dropping off their luggage and without taking even a drop of water at Auntie's home, they headed for the Hanuman temple at Connaught Place in the same taxi, as promised earlier in the day.

That night he felt he had a new lease of life. Kashmir appeared to be a nightmare from a distant past!

He felt he was absolutely *azaad* (free)! He was free of angry demonstrations and slogans, frequent shutdowns, and targeted shootings and bomb blasts. That is what *azaadi* (freedom) meant to him!

Although the Delhi air was not as clean as the Srinagar air, but it was not as tension-filled; he could breathe freely again nearly after a year and a half. He could also eat and sleep without much tension. Most importantly, as a peaceful and responsible citizen of the world, he could focus on the essentials of life and make his positive contribution to the world at large. What else did a man or a woman need?

# The Years Before the Exit

*There could be numerous causes to give our life for, but there is not a single cause to take somebody's life for.
We have only one life, it is best that we try to preserve it and help as many people in the world as possible to preserve theirs and their loved ones.*

—Bill K Koul

**March 1988**
Billu had just completed his Master's Degree in Civil Engineering from the University of Roorkee (known as IIT Roorkee since 2001) with First Class Honours. In March 1988, he returned to Srinagar along with Rekha and their nine-month-old son, Baba (aka Kongposh).

Having been away from his home and his native environment and climatic conditions for more than a year he was very glad to be back in Srinagar. In comparison to Roorkee, Srinagar felt much colder than how it had felt in the past, possibly because of his acclimatisation with the Roorkee weather over all those months. Thankfully, he did not have to again experience those hot and humid days in the forthcoming summer.

Life was once again back in paradise, so it seemed. The 25-year-old buzzed with confidence and excitement about his possible life ahead. He was back home in Kashmir, in the company of his parents. He had a nice respectable job and a loving family. What else did a person need?

Fresh from an upgrade in his technical qualifications, he re-joined his workplace, REC Srinagar (now, NIT Srinagar), as Lecturer in Civil Engineering. His confidence as a teacher had remarkably increased. Plus, as a specialist geotechnical engineer now, he also joined the Geotechnical Engineering Consultancy team in the Civil Engineering department, headed by Prof P N Kachroo, who had been one of his favourite teachers as a student, and subsequently his mentor when he had joined the REC in March 1984 as a teacher. Prof Kachroo had strongly encouraged him to specialise in Geotechnical Engineering.

His workplace was like another home to him. It was like a large family. The family elders comprised all his earlier professors. Amongst them, Professor Barkat Hussain had been his father's classmate at Punjab Engineering College (PEC), Chandigarh. Professor Hussain was also an active member of the consultancy team. Professor R L Misri had been his father's batch mate in FSc (Faculty of Science, now Year 12). Being specialised in Hydraulics, he was not a member of the consultancy team. Professor M K Magazine was distantly related to his in-laws.

Most of his best friends at REC were older than him by four to five years. These included Abdul Rub Shah (who had also been his teacher), Ashok Kaul (Pahalwan) and Rajinder Braroo. In addition, six of his colleagues in the Civil Engineering department had been his classmates during his undergraduate years (1978 to 1983). Many lecturers in other engineering disciplines had also been his batch mates and were his friends now.

Both Abdul Rub and Ashok were graduates from PEC (Chandigarh). They had been teachers at REC in Civil and Mechanical engineering, respectively, from around the time when Billu was a third year student in Civil Engineering. He had, therefore, known them over several years. However, Rajinder, a graduate of Patiala College, had joined the Civil Engineering department several months after Billu. Being entirely new to the college, Rajinder did not have many friends or acquaintances in the college; so Billu had made special endeavours to make him feel welcome and comfortable in the department, which had developed into friendship between the two.

A remarkable feature of his job was that it was non-transferable. In addition, as bonus, REC closed for summer and winter vacations, which allowed one to travel and explore places. Furthermore, career wise, there were continuous opportunities to keep upgrading one's technical knowledge.

Another important characteristic of his job as an academic, which suited his personal temperament, was that he was answerable and required to report mainly to his students and to the Head of his department, and, if required, the college Principal. Thankfully, unlike his peers in government jobs, he did not have to keep the politicians and bureaucrats happy. After a day's work, he could sleep well during the night.

As icing on the cake, he earned his bread through hard work and by honest means; there was no scope or need to do anything otherwise. As a Lecturer, thanks to the UGC, his salary was comparable to an Executive Engineer in the state government at that time. In addition, through regular consultancy, his monthly income was almost two times his monthly salary. The consultancy team provided regular service to the Central

PWD, Indian Army, Border Security Force, Indian Airforce, Kashmir Tourism Department and many other state government and private clients. It was a very satisfying experience to work together and brush shoulders with a wide range of practicing engineers across the industry.

A number of college staff buses, with a distinct maroon band, painted with REGIONAL ENGINEERING COLLEGE SRINAGAR in white enamel paint, provided transport to the REC employees between the college and other parts of the Srinagar city. These buses stood out from the common buses due to their unique appearances.

Unlike other RECs in India, the Srinagar REC remained open on Saturdays, but closed after midday on Fridays. Every now and then, especially on a Friday afternoon, Billu and one of his best friends would alight from the bus near Radio Kashmir Station and walk to Lal Chowk on Bund which runs along River Jhelum.

On reaching the General Post Office (GPO), they would enter Tao Café, located not far from the GPO. The café is housed in a small country style cottage, nestled between Residency Road and the Bund, located adjacent to a wide stairway connecting the two. It may have been established around mid to late 1979 or so. At its full capacity, the café could accommodate about 50 people; two-thirds of those in its outdoor picturesque setting within a number of old Chinar trees.

One of the waiters at the café was Riyaz, a pleasing young lad, around 21 years old in 1989. He was very amicable, with good etiquette, and provided prompt service with a smile. Being a vegetarian, Billu would usually eat panner pakora and vegetarian Chinese cuisine at the café. Riyaz did not need to be told what to serve; he knew what to serve on the day.

During the summer of 1988, Billu visited the café numerous times, usually on Friday afternoons but also occasionally after work on long summer days between June to August. On many such occasions, Ashok was his companion. Usually over tea at the café, they would discuss their plan to start a new engineering college in Srinagar. Incidentally, Ashok had also been discussing the plan with another colleague of theirs, Kuldeep Bhat, a Lecturer at that time in Mechanical Engineering at the REC.

Ashok belonged to a relatively affluent family from Rajbagh. He was a handsome and good looking fellow. In general social conversations, he would come across as a very relaxed and a broadminded person, usually with a typical smile on his face. Although Billu was about four to five years younger than him, they clicked well, possibly due to their common relaxed and broadminded personalities, despite considerable differences in their engineering disciplines, backgrounds, and personal food and drink preferences. Unlike mainstream Kashmiris, he and Billu shared a number of common interests. Both liked to read non-fiction and science fiction, listen to western music and watch western movies, buy good clothes and wear nice shoes. On a regular basis, they would temporarily swap books and vinyl records (LP, SP). The two did not like to indulge in any social or political gossip. In addition to their plans for starting a new engineering college, they also generally talked about their desire to play golf at the Srinagar Golf Club.

Their other regular places of interest along Residency Road were:

> Subhana the Best Tailors, adjacent to Bund off Residency Road. Over the last decade or so, on an average at least once every month, Billu had been a regular customer of the shop.
> Shakti Sweets, located near Regal Cinema. It was a busy Indian snack shop. On some days, after work, Billu would go there in the company of Rajinder or Ashok.
> Lica Studios, located adjacent to Shakti Sweets. He visited the shop frequently, almost once every fortnight to purchase photo films and print photographs.

Dimples' ice cream parlour, located across the road, opposite Lica Studios. Bata Shoe shop, located adjacent to Dimples' ice cream parlour. Ashok and he used to purchase footwear from there on an average one pair every month. In 1988, they bought three pairs each, same style but different sizes. Master Arts, a fantastic garment shop, located opposite Partap Park. Billu still has some woollen sweaters from his Kashmir days which are in a top notch condition.

Radio Light, located near the Information Centre, opposite Partap Park. Billu would visit the shop at least once or twice a week and browse through the stack of vinyl records (LP, SP, EP) to check for the new arrivals. Those days, vinyl records were relatively expensive; each about Rupees 50 to 75. In addition to Radio Light, he would also buy records from an HMV shop, located across the Amira Kadal Bridge, opposite Jehangir Hotel. Erina Ice Cream parlour, located adjacent to Radio Light. Sant Ram Sweets, located in the congested part of Lal Chowk area.

Broadway cinema was always an attraction for its outstanding acoustics and sound system. In addition, Billu watched movies at Regal and Palladium cinemas, especially if a western movie was being screened, in particular, starring Clint Eastwood or Charles Bronson or for that matter any movie that depicted World War II.

Those were the days! Life was nice, relatively simpler and easier, and without much fuss. In addition, he did not have to find and pay for a separate house to live in. He used a major portion of his income in meeting the necessary living expenses of his young family. Although Boba looked after most of the day-to-day expenses at home, as a responsible and self-respecting son, Billu regularly provided a complimentary supporting hand, although nothing was demanded or expected by his parents.

In April 1988, when Billu and Ashok discussed their plans and blueprints for a new engineering college, hardly did they know that a mega-scale blueprint was being prepared elsewhere for their homeland. They had no idea about what was being hatched in the living rooms of their Kashmiri brethren and the trouble which imminently brewed on the horizon. Obviously, the memories of the 1985-86 uprising in Anantnag had faded away in their mind. Although the vegetable and fruit vendors, as well as most grocers, some bus-conductors and many labourers had started to allude to the idea that Kashmir would soon resemble Palestine, they did not pay any serious attention to such comments. Such speculations were nothing new for them. In short, they did not have even a sniff of an organised and accelerated momentum that had been imparted to a separatist militant movement in Kashmir post the 1985-86 uprising in Anantnag.

Although people had started to hear about the movements of some new separatist leaders, Billu, and many people with whom he regularly interacted, had no clue about a considerable number of Kashmiris undertaking well-coordinated and organised secessionist activities.

In May 1988, Billu and Rekha joined a group of friends on a two-day excursion at Gulmarg and Tangmarg. At Gulmarg, which is about 56 km from Srinagar, they stayed at the BARC (Bhaba Atomic Research Centre) guesthouse for one night. Gulmarg, which stands at a minimum altitude of about 2,650 m above the mean sea level, is characterised by beautiful natural meadows. It has amongst the highest natural golf courses in the world. Next day, they picnicked at the picturesque Tangmarg, located at foothills of Gulmarg, about 40 km from Srinagar. At Tangmarg, they camped on the bank of a beautiful stream. Looking back, it was a very precious and memorable trip. The male members of the group, all medical doctors by profession, comprised Dr M L Pandit (brother-in-law through his marriage), Dr Kishore Kampassi, Dr Chand Wattal and Dr Kamlesh Deewani.

Between 9 and 14 June 1988, for a period of five days, a violent agitation was witnessed in Srinagar over a proposed increase in the power tariff. The agitation caused significant disturbance to the life of a common man. This was seemingly the first prolonged disturbing activity that brought life in the valley to a virtual standstill. Possibly, there may have been a link between the secessionist movement and this agitation, but most Pandits, including Billu, had no clue about any such link. Things were still seen based on only their face value.

In June 1988, the Koul family participated actively in a number of weddings. In practical terms, life still felt relatively secure and normal at this stage, although some social murmur and whispers about the possibility of something happening had grown steadily in the past few months. Rekha's and Baba's first birthdays were celebrated in the third and fourth week of June 1988. Auntie and her children visited Kashmir and stayed with the Koul family.

Little did anyone see at that time that the storm clouds were actually gathering on the horizon and that such tranquil days would not last very long!

During the 2-week summer college break in July 1988 and after Auntie's departure to Delhi, Billu and his family went for an excursion to Daksum. They were accompanied by Gashaji and his family. Rekha's younger sister, Puja, and a cousin from Delhi, Sangeeta Kachroo, who was visiting her maternal family in Srinagar, also accompanied them. Billu thus led a large team, comprising four adults and five children, to that excursion without any fear whatsoever. They enjoyed themselves in the jungles of the picturesque Daksum area. They were blissfully oblivious of the activities being undertaken by the secessionists elsewhere!

On 31 July 1988, out of the blue, two bomb blasts rocked Srinagar city, one at the Central Telegraph Office and one near the Srinagar Golf Club area. Reportedly, both were carried out by the activists of a separatist militant organisation.

The bomb blasts marked the beginning of armed militancy in the valley.

People suddenly became apprehensive about an armed movement. Now with greater confidence, many shopkeepers openly started warning their customers that Kashmir would soon become like Palestine. Interestingly, before these bomb blasts, Billu had never taken such warnings and speculations seriously.

The social murmur and whispers about an armed uprising suddenly became louder. People said that a considerable number of Kashmiri youth had crossed over to Pakistan and had now returned after receiving training in the use of arms and ammunitions.

Blissfully, the Pandit community enjoyed the psychological assurance that, due to the presence of a large contingent of Indian Army in the Valley, the uprising would not be very serious. The Pandit elders tried to reconcile to the situation using their own outdated logic and reassured their younger generations that nothing untoward was going to happen. To support their arguments,, they generally used the outcome of the numerous past disturbances in the valley, such as the Pakistani Kabaili Raid in October 1947 and the Batamalloo infiltration episode of August 1965. One Pandit elder said to Billu, 'Son, please don't worry. We have seen these things happening since our childhood. Nothing major is going to happen. Our Muslim brothers will not allow infliction of any harm on us. And, we also have army here, so don't worry. It is normal!'

As history proved, the Pandit elders had completely misread the situation in 1989; their thinking was compromised due to a number of factors, including unreasonable reliance on the Indian government and, to a great extent, their own inertia.

In August 1988, the family celebrated Billu's birthday. Billu proposed a 3-day excursion at Verinag, which Boba agreed to. After booking a tourist hut, they reached Verinag in the early afternoon of 17 August 1988. Puja and Sangeeta were also with them. During the day, they had an enjoyable time. However, around 9 pm, when the family was preparing to leave for dinner in the dining area, Boba's driver, Muhammed Shafi, knocked at the door of their hut. He looked pale and disturbed. He said that the then President of Pakistan, General Zia-ul-Haq, had been killed in an air crash, and strongly advised that the family should leave for Srinagar in the early hours of the morning. He anticipated serious law and order situation across the valley. Everyone became extremely worried and nervous. No one ate dinner that night. Ladies and the girls did not even change their clothes for fear of retribution and/or a possibility of having to escape at short notice. It was an extremely tense night.

The next morning, they started very early from Verinag. Muhammed Shafi was right. The scenario along the road looked tense. Despite leaving early, they had to take shelter in the Dak Bungalow at Khanabal, due to curfew and violent incidents of rioting in the area. They heard the news about wide-spread anti-India and anti-government demonstrations being staged on all roads leading to Srinagar and spent a tense day at the Khanabal Dak Bungalow before nervously leaving for Srinagar in the evening. Everyone aboard the vehicle was tense, given that it was a government vehicle. After passing through some potentially dangerous areas, fortunately they reached home unharmed. Thereafter, the city remained disturbed and tense for a number of days. Anti-India slogans were loud on the streets.

The ficklemindedness of a typical Kashmiri Muslim is a distinct and notable characteristic. The protestors and violent agitators were the same people who had also previously shouted anti General Zia-ul-Haq slogans when Zulfikar Ali Bhutto was hanged on 4 April 1979. So, the question arises, 'How did General Zia-ul-Haq win the loyalty of Kashmiri Muslims within nine years without even stepping his foot in the valley?' The answer to this question is a key to the solution of the Kashmir issue.

After the earlier twin bomb blasts in July 1988, a number of militancy related incidents took place in the valley. On 11 and 12 September 1988, the Srinagar city was again tense. It was said that a number of Pakistan trained militants had reportedly been arrested.

Ashok was married in September 1988. Most of the staff of REC Srinagar attended the wedding reception at his Rajbagh residence.

On the night of 17 and 18 September 1988, some militants attacked the Rajbagh residence of DIG Kashmir range, Ali Muhammad Watali, who escaped unhurt. However, in the retaliatory action, Aijaz Dar, a militant was reportedly killed by the security forces. An automatic sophisticated firearm was recovered from him at the encounter site, which confirmed the birth of a serious armed movement in Kashmir. The daring attack on the DIG provided a taste of things to come. The news spread across Kashmir in no time, like wildfire.

Despite all above militant incidents, general life continued to be more or less normal; albeit regular calls for *bundh* (a general shut down) disturbed the normal life. Strong rumours about the ongoing militant activities were, however, rife towards the end of 1988.

As Kashmir prepared to settle for harsh winter months ahead, REC Srinagar closed for the usual winter break. Similar to the previous years, Billu and his family flew to Delhi towards the end of December 1988 and the family settled down to enjoy the warmer months at Delhi.

Despite their physical absence from the valley, disturbing news from the state never stopped arriving, which made Billu a bit worried. From a distance, he saw some kind of a strange pattern in several incidents, which took place on a regular (almost fortnightly) basis. To start with, unprecedented Hindu-Sikh riots took place in Jammu city on 13 January 1989 on the birthday of Guru Gobind Singhji, which was followed by Kashmiri people marking the Republic Day of India (26 January) as 'Black Day'. About two weeks later, widespread violence erupted again in Kashmir on 11 February 1989, the death anniversary of Maqbool Butt, a separatist. Widespread violence again engulfed the valley after some time as a reaction against Salman Rushdie's book, notwithstanding the fact that the book had been banned in India. This reaction paralysed the valley for nearly five days.

Besides being fickle minded, typical Kashmiri Muslims are also extremely sensitive and reactive to any incident in the world. To get excited and angry, they only need a rumour.

There seemed to be a qualitative change in the pattern of violence after January 1989. Sophisticated firearms and explosives brought a new unprecedented era into the valley. Targeted bomb blasts were carried out to create an atmosphere of tension and panic amongst the public.

The first quarter of the Year 1989 (and the following months) saw a series of regular calls for agitations and shutdowns by various political and separatist groups. Although the calls were given by the individual groups, it seemed all groups were well coordinated and endorsed by all known militant formations.

The Koul family returned to Srinagar in the second week of March 1989. REC Srinagar had opened about a week ago. Billu resumed his work. In early April 1989, the family accompanied their doctor friends on a day excursion at Prang; about 12 km to the east of the central hub of district Ganderbal.

Tuesday, 18 April 1989, was a dark day for Billu and REC Srinagar. Ashok Kaul passed away that day in a tragic road accident. Around 10 am on Wednesday, 19 April 1989, the shocking news of Ashok's death on the previous day spread through the college like wildfire. Just a few days ago they had been to Tao Café and had also shopped together on Residency Road. Billu was stunned and had to rush to the toilet and threw up. A significant part of him died with Ashok on that morning.

A number of violent incidents also occurred during that month for nearly a week to represent the public reaction against the arrest of (militant) Kashmiri youth by the police.

On 10 May 1989, still recovering from Ashok's death, Billu accompanied Rekha (and Baba) to Jammu to attend her cousin's wedding. They were part of a bigger family group that travelled from Srinagar by an 18-seater Swaraj Mazda minibus.

The 4-day Quit Kashmir Movement, launched by a prominent secessionist militant group in Kashmir, from 11 to 14 May 1989, coincided with his Jammu trip. Although the news was concerning to everyone and people did discuss this development in Jammu during the wedding ceremony, it had little impact on Billu, perhaps because he was away from the scene. Out of sight, out of mind!

In early June 1989, one evening Billu experienced some heart palpitation during a severe thunderstorm. He and his family got worried. The next day, he went to his family doctor, Dr Sarup, at Rawalpora. Dr Sarup advised him that there was nothing to worry about; his palpitations could have been caused by heartburn, possibly as a result of a disturbed state of his mind triggered by militant activities. It also seemed Ashok's untimely death may have precipitated his heartburn.

Sometime in the middle of the month, they joined the faculty of Civil Engineering department, headed by Professsor Kachroo, and their families on a day excursion at Prang.

In the first week of July 1989, Baba's *zarkasay* ceremony (the first-hair cutting ceremony) was performed at the Ksheer Bhawani shrine, in Tulmul. As his hair was being cut for the first time, Baba cried a lot when he saw thick golden brown locks of his curly hair falling on the tiled floor. Billu remembered his own *zarkasay*, which had also been performed at the same place in the summer of 1969, exactly 20 years ago. He missed Amaji, as she had on her own performed his *zarkasay*.

After a week or so, as a group leader of a young engineering faculty, Billu accompanied the students of Civil Engineering on an educational one-day excursion at the scenic meadows of Yusmarg. Rekha and Baba accompanied him. It was a day full of fun. Baba became very popular with his father's colleagues and the students. On the way, the family stopped by at Charar-e-Sharief shrine to pay their respects there.

The first organised attack on para-military forces was carried out by the militants on 13 July 1989, when three CRPF personnel were killed in Srinagar. The militant attacks did not help Billu. His mental condition deteriorated further. The frequency of his heartburn increased, as did his belching to relieve himself of stomach gases.

Billu's mental state deteriorated a few further notches when relatives considered him as an enemy, sadly for no personal rhyme or reason. Around that time in Srinagar, the word 'enemy' carried a potential threat to one's life. As far as he knew, Billu did not know anyone from within the Muslim community who could regard him as his enemy. But now, out of the blue, he had an enemy and that too from within his own community. It was a person who did not know him at all but seemingly hated him the most.

Billu felt compromised by his relatives. First his best friend, Ashok, was gone and now he had a personal enemy. In addition, the situation in Kashmir deteriorated day by day. He lost appetite and could not sleep well during the nights. He was well and truly gripped by fear for his life. He feared death due to a sudden heart attack or due to a random bomb blast or getting caught in a cross fire. Dr Sarup sent him for ECG testing and the results came back as normal. It seemed he suffered from anxiety and depression disorder. Dr Sarup prescribed him some tranquilisers and anti-depressants and advised him to run every day for five to six kilometres. The militant activities in the Valley acquired a significant momentum in the second half of 1989. The first political killing was carried out by the militants on 7 August 1989 when Mohd Yusuf Halwai, Block President National Conference was killed. The violent incidents of August were followed by a series of explosions in parts of the Srinagar city during September 1989.

On 14 September 1989, Pandit Tika Lal Taploo, an advocate by profession and a prominent leader of the Pandit community, on both social and political fronts, was killed by the militants in broad-day light, in front of his own house and in the presence of eyewitnesses. Kashmiris, in particular, the Pandit community in Kashmir was shocked beyond words. Pandit Taploo's intentional and targeted killing instilled deep fear in the Pandit community. The killers were never apprehended and, therefore, the Pandit community did not feel safe in the valley any longer.

The militants and secessionists had successfully torn apart the traditional social structure in Kashmir and seriously dented its foundations, which had stood through centuries on mutual love, faith, trust and brotherhood between the two communities.

On 4 January 1990, a local Urdu newspaper, *Aftab*, published a press release by Hizb-ul-Mujahideen, asking Pandits to leave the valley. The expulsion order was also published in another local paper, *Al Safa*. Explosive and inflammatory speeches were broadcast from PA systems at the mosques on the night between 19 and 20 January 1990, which triggered the mass exodus of Pandits from the valley in the following days and weeks.

Militants also abducted and threatened civilians for extortion. Members of some of the militant groups committed rape; threatened and attacked journalists and kidnapped tourists and other prominent people as political hostages.

The shocking assassinations made a significant impact on Billu's mind. None of the previous militant attacks was carried out on any member of the Pandit community. He became afraid, very afraid.

One day in late September 1989, Boba returned from work earlier than his usual time and asked Billu to ask Khazar Mohammed (head mason) to come and see Boba in connection with the construction of a new bathroom in the second storey of the house. Billu refused to go, saying, 'I am sorry, I won't go to call him. I don't want you to waste your money on the construction of this new bathroom. You know, the situation is not improving in Kashmir. All Pandits will have to leave their home one day and move out of Kashmir. You will also have to leave this home one day. That day, remember my words, the close proximity of the airport will prove to be of great help to you. Please don't construct the bathroom. If you still don't understand what I am saying and want to go ahead, then you may go and see him yourself. I don't want to be a party to this. Sorry.' As usual, Boba did not believe him and brushed him off. He was visibly disappointed to hear his son's words. Then, Boba left home himself to see Khazar Mohammad.

One Saturday evening in early October 1989, Billu begged of his parents that he should be allowed to leave Kashmir and go to Delhi, as he was really struggling with the deteriorating conditions in Srinagar. His parents tried to dissuade him on the pretext of his job being in Srinagar and the uncertainty in regard to his future in Delhi. Somehow, they agreed. Due to fewer flights those days and a short notice period, the earliest tickets were available for Monday. Billu bought the air tickets for himself and his young family. On Sunday morning, he called Rajinder and requested him for a meeting. Rajinder did not live very far from Billu's home. They sat outside in the lawn and had tea. During their chat, they discussed the college and the overall deteriorated security scenario in Srinagar.

Billu said, 'Rajinder, on Monday afternoon, I am leaving for Delhi with Rekha and Baba. I feel very unsafe here. I am not feeling very well and I can't sleep. I'll try to find a job for myself in Delhi.

'My parents don't listen to me. My father-in-law also does not believe me. They all say that they have seen such things happening in Kashmir since they were young. No one believes me. People seem to think I am a mental case, no one has ever said anything but I can see that thought in their eyes. Eyes reveal a person's mind.

'Our Muslim friends and colleagues seem to have changed over all these months. Their handshake doesn't feel as warm and firm as it used to be a year ago. Even their smiles don't look very genuine. Haven't you noticed when you enter the staff room or anyone's office, they suddenly stop chatting, rather whispering, and wait for you to leave the room to resume their chat/whisper? Have you not noticed that they have lately started chatting with one another in a very hushed down tone? I think, they definitely know something that we don't know, my friend; they definitely know something is going to happen soon.'

Rajinder looked a bit bemused and replied, 'Kuldeep, I concur fully with your observations and thoughts. Perhaps, we are not very safe here; militant activities seem to be ramping up quite fast. But tell me, my friend, where shall I go? You can live with your aunt in Delhi till you can find a job; you have been living with her for up to couple of months every winter. But, my friend, where shall I live? Unlike you, I don't have a caring relative outside Kashmir. My wife has a good job here. We are settled here. My parents live with us. They will not be able to survive outside Kashmir in that climatically hot environment. My mother is physically quite weak.

'Every brick of our house is as good as gold. It has been constructed out of our sweat and blood. It contains my father's entire retirement gratuity as well as all my savings from Iraq. Every penny that I have earned after my graduation is cast into my house. Believe me; I have worked very hard in private engineering companies since my graduation. Unlike government jobs, one has to toil very hard to survive in private companies.

'I left my sick mother in Kashmir in care of my father and younger brother years back and went overseas to earn some quick money for the family in Iraq; otherwise we could not have constructed this house. It was not easy for me to leave my mother for all these years. I felt guilty every moment I lived away from her. She is so fragile, you know that. But things had to be done. It, therefore, contains my sacrifice and the sacrifice of my family. If I leave Kashmir, I must also carry my house on wheels. Is that possible? My house is my mother's temple. It is our sweat and blood. We can't simply uproot ourselves and flee from our home.'

'Shall I look for a job for you as well once I am in Delhi?' Billu asked.

'Yes, you may, let us see', Rajinder replied with not much conviction in his voice.

Billu wrote a leave application and requested Rajinder to submit it in the office and personally explain to the Head of Civil Engineering Department why he had to leave suddenly for Delhi. Billu had not taken prior permission to leave the station.

Interestingly, Rajinder was the only person who had agreed with Billu so far as the deteriorating situation in Kashmir was concerned, as well as Billu's perceptions about the people's changed behaviour and their intriguing body language. However, like all others, Rajinder was prepared to brave the storm and stay put where he was.

On Monday, Billu and his young family boarded the first flight to Delhi. As soon as he landed in Delhi, he felt so much better and safe. Delhi appeared to be much brighter than the gloomy days in Srinagar. The family took a taxi at the airport and drove straight to Auntie's place. Since 1973, Billu had been living with her for two months every winter.

During the next couple of days, Billu relaxed and got some sleep. In Srinagar, he had not been sleeping well despite the medication. His hunger for food also gradually returned. After a few days, he and Auntie started talking to people about his job prospects. One of Auntie's colleagues recommended that he should apply to Kirloskars, a leading engineering company in India.

Billu also visited the home of his first cousin. Her father-in-law Brij Lal Sadhu took personal interest in helping Billu. Over a number of visits, each time over lunch, he personally drafted a new version of Billu's CV to make it attractive enough for a prospective employer. In addition, he also drafted a decent job application for him and provided him with a list of prospective employers, along with encouragement and useful tips. Billu also learnt that, in addition to the Saturday or Sunday newspapers, he should purchase the Wednesday issue of *Times of India*, which advertised the most engineering job positions. The draft application and the CV prepared by Brij Lalji retrospectively stood Billu in good stead.

Billu also met Shiban Krishan Bhan, another relative who said, 'Delhi or Detroit, it is the same thing once you are out of Kashmir. Why slog in Delhi if you can manage to find better opportunities in a developed country? Please don't waste your time here, go overseas.' His words proved to be prophetic.

After a week or so, Boba called Billu over phone and advised that he should return to REC and wait till the end of December when it closed for the winter break. It was only a matter of two more months. Billu agreed to return to Srinagar, based on a painful realisation that he had not been successful in finding any substantial means of sustenance yet in Delhi. How long could he and his family stay with Auntie? He was no more single. It was not right for him to prolong his stay. In addition, he was fast running out of cash that he had brought from Srinagar. After two weeks in Delhi, they returned to Srinagar with a heavy heart. His fear psychosis and its biological manifestations returned very quickly.

In the last quarter of 1989, the agitations increased and were characterised by spontaneity. The violent incidents became extensive and also affected the rural areas, although Srinagar remained the focus of violence. On 4 November 1989, a group of three militants shot dead Judge Neel Kanth Ganjoo in broad day-light, as he was walking in the Hari Singh Street market near the High Court in Srinagar.

By now, the Pandit community was convinced that prominent persons belonging to the community were being specifically targeted and annihilated by the militants to scare the community in order to complete their mission whatever it was.

Billu's mental conditions took a further dive. His eldest aunt, Behanji, advised him to visit Sai'd sahib's shrine for spiritual blessings, which he did. He also met Swami Vishud Chaitnya at Bohri Kadal for assistance in relieving him of his fear psychosis, who gave him a *Rudrakh* and *yantra* to keep under his pillow for better sleep. He was given black pepper kernels to eat on a regular basis. He started chanting Hanuman

Chalisa daily and always carried a small size copy of *Hanuman Chalisa* in his pocket.

Rubaiya Sayeed, daughter of Mufti Mohammed Sayeed, the then Union Home Minister, was abducted in Srinagar on 8 December 1989. Five hard-core JKLF militants were released from jail on 13 December 1989 in exchange of Dr Rubaiya Sayeed's release.

Following a significant rise in the intensity of militant activities, political assassinations and intimidation of political opponents, traditional political parties appeared to have become practically ineffective, inactive and marginalised. The fire seemed to have gone out of control. Everyone seemed to live in fear, as collateral damages were real possibilities.

In December 1989, nearly every time Billu belched, his pulse remained always fast, more than 120 beats per minute. Heart palpitations had become a normal experience. He hardly slept. Food did not taste anything at all; he never felt hungry and it was an effort to eat. He walked with a bent gait. Sunshine irritated him. He felt so insecure that he (and Rekha) shared his parent's large second-storey bedroom for sleeping. He did not attend any social or wedding functions. His outdoor movements became limited to only engaging classes at REC. Mentally, he became so crippled that Rekha had to accompany him to his workplace. She would wait for him at the Hazrtabal Shrine while he would take his classes at the REC. He hardly opened the lock of his personal office room. After his classes, he would walk quietly and quickly visit the Shrine to join her and return home. REC closed for winter vacations in the third week of December 1989.

Billu left the valley on 23 December 1989, accompanied by Rekha and Baba. Had he lost his paradise for ever?

Even on that day, except Rajinder, no one else appeared to understand what he was saying and how he was suffering.

Aboard the flight, he thought, 'What is wrong with the people; why can't they perceive what has been quite obvious to me? How much thick is their skin? Are they fools? Aren't the Pandits supposed to be wise and intelligent? But, hold on, what if I was completely wrong in judging the situation and making predictions about a mass exodus of Pandits from Kashmir?' As history unfolded in the coming few weeks, Billu's fear was vindicated. He had not been wrong.

With his fragile state of mind, at the time of his exit from Kashmir, Billu was mentally too sick to understand why other people did not openly express their feelings and react to the situation in Kashmir as he had done during the last crippling months of 1989. A few months after the mass exodus of his community in January 1990, he found the answer himself when he had recovered sufficiently.

The inertial position of the Pandits in the pre-1990 era, so as it had seemed to Billu, could be explained by science as well as by philosophy. For example, as per Newton's First Law of Motion, *an object continues to remain at rest or continues to stay in motion at a constant velocity in a straight line, unless acted upon by a net force.* Accordingly, the behaviour of all objects can be described by saying that objects tend to 'keep on doing what they're doing', unless acted upon by an *unbalanced force*. Therefore, if at rest, the object will continue to be in the same state of rest. All objects resist changes in their state of motion; they tend to 'keep on doing what they're doing'.

Man (both woman and man) is known to resist change. We don't like changes; we like to stick to the routine. Kashmiri Pandits were no different. And, this was a change like no other. After the final departure from this world, what could be the next biggest change for a man (and a woman) other than having to leave his (and her) home where all his (and her) ancestors were born and thrived till they had departed from the world? Their mortal remains had become part of the soil which had given birth to the generation that had followed them.

Unless a situation is potentially catastrophic, where one's life and honour is at stake, people generally adopt an ostrich like attitude. Similarly, the Pandits had nowhere to go. All their ancestors had lived there. People don't uproot themselves and abandon their homes. Kashmir was their home. They had hoped for the best and, in doing so, they simply ignored the future possibilities, howsoever inevitable these possibilities actually were. One could say they had self-hypnotised themselves.

As history unfolded on the night of 19 January 1990, the community suddenly woke up from that state of self-hypnosis, as the loud speakers screamed that shocking message for them, loud and clear. They had to pull their head out of the sand and flee for their lives and honour.

As per Newton's Third Law, *when one body exerts a force on a second body, the second body simultaneously exerts a force equal in magnitude and opposite in direction on the first body.* As Pandits had no means to exert the equal and opposite force, the *unbalanced force* resulted in the change of their direction through an aperture/vent called the Banihal tunnel. Given that they have been known to be *Dal-e-Bhattas*, a slurry-like fluid, their behaviour was similar to fluids. What happens to a fluid when a force is exerted on it in a confined space? It escapes through any vent/space that is available to it. Had Pandits not been so tenacious, resilient and fluid-like flexible, they could not have survived so long in the valley. Not being solids was their strength and the means for survival.

As for Billu, he had an easier choice. To flee, unlike most others. Unlike Rajinder, he had not constructed his own house through his hard earned money. The house that he lived in belonged to his father. So, Billu did not have the same level of attachment with his father's house as Rajinder had with his own house. Plus, he had a base in Delhi, which not many Pandits had outside Kashmir. And also, he was very familiar with the climatic and living conditions outside Kashmir after having lived in Delhi and Roorkee.

He also realised that, on that day in October 1989, Rajinder had actually vented the thoughts and feelings of any Pandit living in the valley at that time. This only goes to prove the extreme level of desperation which Pandits must have experienced that had forced them to flee their home suddenly after January 1990. Otherwise, they had been so resilient and tenacious all along that they would never have abandoned their homes. Only an upheaval could have made them desperate enough to flee.

Was Billu selfish in the sense that he left his parents and his young girl cousin in the valley and moved to a relatively safer place about a month before the mass exodus of his community? Didn't he care for his parents and his cousin? Perhaps, there was an element of selfishness in his action, so it would seem if seen from the surface. But looking deeply, he had done everything that he could. He had made lots of noise over several months. His father was a relatively young man, not even 50 at that time, with responsibilities of a senior government servant. Not actually believing Billu, he had ended up spending a significant amount of money in the construction of his new second-storey bathroom at a time when his son was struggling with mental agony.

Considering how much noise Billu had made, about '*something wrong and terrible was happening around or going to happen*' with his elders, friends and relatives, and most of his colleagues at work, Billu was quite fortunate to have left Kashmir relatively physically unscathed, notwithstanding the fact he was mentally quite bruised and severally battered.

Not so long after he left Kashmir in December 1989, any person making such noise could have been physically targeted by the armed militants because the secessionists would have easily mistaken him for an Indian intelligence agent and misconstrued his noise. They would have inferred that he definitely knew something about their movement. His noise was not obviously beneficial for maintaining the element of surprise that they had kept up their sleeves, to launch their movement, which they did finally on the night of 19 January 1990.

Who would have bothered to find out that he was making noise purely out of his gut feeling and premonition, without having any evidence about anything?

Personally, Billu had not seen or heard anything from the secessionists. He had no proof. His feeling was purely based on his sensitivity. He had successfully deciphered the meaning of (a) bomb blasts; (b) targeted assassinations; and (c) frequent agitations, and correlated them with (a) a sudden loss of firmness in handshake with his colleagues; (b) sudden disappearance of hugs; (c) avoidance of eye contact during one-to-one conversations with his friends and colleagues; (d) rumours at his workplace combined with comments and remarks made by his colleagues from time to time with elements of subtle sarcasm.

Everything seemed to fit in with what shopkeepers and bus conductors had been saying for quite some time, *'this place will become like Palestine one day'*. His sensitive nature and the habit of paying close attention to details did not miss an obvious significant change in the pattern of the human behaviour around him, although subtle. He was too thin-skinned to have missed what was happening around him. His sensitivity worked both ways; it alarmed him in the very early days of the militant uprising and scared him to leave in advance of most of his community, but it also took a very heavy toll on his mental health at that time.

After 19 January 1990, most Pandit families left Kashmir one by one and moved to many places which were unfamiliar to the most, such as Jammu, Delhi, Pune and other places.

Most people, especially the elderly, did not possess the necessary survival skills, whatsoever, about how to deal with the heat and the snake bites, which retrospectively killed hundreds of them. How many people died of shock!

One can only cry at the sheer desperation of this community. Even God must have cried each time a family would have left their home, with hearts pounding, with sadness and tears flowing down their eyes, for an uncertain and unknown future, leaving everything behind. It is deeply heartrending even to imagine how a Pandit mother, grandmother and/or a great-grandmother must have sighed *vaey* (a painful moan) while stepping outside their house for the last time. Every *vaey* of theirs may have possibly cracked and burst a big rock somewhere on the earth.

Traditionally, Pandits would do *namaskar* to their house when they would leave for a journey or a pilgrimage. It is not very hard to imagine how wet their eyes would have been when they bid their last parting goodbye, with folded hands, to their home and hearth.

Billu has tried to dispel a myth about the reasons underlying the mass exodus of the Pandit community, that has been created and nurtured over the years in Kashmir by the Muslim community. It is said that the Pandits were asked to leave Kashmir by the then Governor of Jammu & Kashmir, Jagmohan.

Our Muslim brethren should know, or may already know that every Pandit considers himself or herself as the most knowledgeable and wise person. It is not easy to convince a Pandit to do something which he/she does not agree to do. Due to their individualistic nature, it is practically impossible to bring the whole Pandit community in the world under one umbrella and one leadership. Every Pandit considers himself/ herself a leader. Would they have listened to Jagmohan to leave even if he would have asked them to leave? They don't follow anyone except themselves. It has been a common knowledge that a brother did not even inform his own brother, who lived in the same house, that he was intending to leave with his family in the early hours of the next morning. Obviously, the only reason that Pandits left was that they felt extremely endangered and insecure and did not really believe that their Muslim brethren will protect them. They had to flee for their lives and honour, and fend for themselves.

What was really their fault for which they had been asked, rather forced, to leave their homes on the night of 19 January 1990?

As humans have been unable to provide a reasonable and true answer so far, one can only hope that God will answer that question one day.

The generations of Pandits who left their home after January 1990 will find it very hard to reconcile; some will find it definitely practically impossible. Now that things have happened, they can't be reversed. Reconciliation is required for healing, which can be done either by a positive and coherent action by both the major Kashmiri communities (Muslims and Pandits) or by a philosophical approach, as defined hereunder.

Colloquially, when we meet an extremely patient and tolerant person, we tell that person, 'You have the patience of a saint'. No surprise that the children of those Rishis and the Saints, after whom Kashmir used to be called the *Reshvear* (the garden of Rishis), showed such immense patience before painfully saying good bye to their home.

It is said that once Baba Guru Nanak Dev visited two villages. The first village was inhabited by people who were generally noble and peace-loving, whereas the people in the second village were a little different. While departing, he said to the people of the first village, *Ujjad jao* (get uprooted), whereas he said *Basee Raho* (stay put and prosper) to the people of the second village. His disciple and assistant, Mardana, was shocked to hear him saying these contradictory words to the two groups of people. Baba Nanak clarified, 'The people in the first village are generally noble and full of goodness. The world will benefit more from them if they disperse throughout the world and spread their goodness around.'

Were Baba Nanak's words prophetic for Kashmiri Pandits? He would know and time will tell! As Kashmiri Pandits are known to be amongst the highest order of Brahmins, their stagnation in the valley was perhaps not acceptable to Mother Nature. They had to keep moving to regain their purity. And look back at the life of a typical Kashmiri family in the valley since the mid-20$^{th}$ century.

May be the higher logic prevailed; only God knows the bigger picture!

# Life in Kashmir

The story begins in 1961. It starts with Billu's parents, their marriage and the subsequent role of the two families in his upbringing.

**Rani**

Rani was a 17-year-old, very pretty, intelligent and an innocent looking young woman. She came from a typical middle class family of Kashmir, albeit hailing from a rich and cultured background. Her father, Pitaji, the only earning member in the family, died suddenly. He was a Tourist Officer and most of his friends were from the UK. He spoke English with a typical British accent.

On Pitaji's demise, the grief-striken family was under constant financial pressures. Rani's mother, Kaki, had to take the brunt of the whole family on her shoulders. Kaki was very fair, soft spoken and beautiful, with silver grey hair. She always wore white sarees. She was a silent worker and an excellent cook. She sang numerous Kashmiri folk songs with a very melodious voice, in particular the songs sung by various popular radio singers of the time, such as Rajabhegum, Zoonbhegum and Asha Kaul.

Rani had an older sister, Benigashi, who lived in Bombay. Benigashi was nearly 14 years older than Rani. She also had a younger sister, Chandrabagha, who was married when Billu was a toddler, and a younger brother, Avtar Krishan (*Boba Maama*). Rani loved Avtar the most. He suffered from ill health from a very young age.

Avtar grew up to become a dentist. He enjoyed a fair bit of success and popularity with patients.

Rani was full of dreams and aspirations, with an open mind and she was a keen learner. She should have been born to royalty. She was unlike most of her contemporaries. Her father led a quintessential English lifestyle, with a typical British accent and smoked cigars. As he worked close to the British, Rani was influenced by the western lifestyle from an early age. She loved to read history and biographies of famous people, in particular, the British royalty. She was also very artistic and skilful in handicrafts such as knitting and crochet.

Rani was very fond of films and songs. She was gifted with a sweet voice but the theme would always be sad, perhaps a reflection of her own mind. She could have easily been a successful actress of her time had she gone to Bombay.

## Boba

Boba was an 18-year-old. Academically, he was a high achiever and one of the best students of his time. Like Rani, he was also second in line of four children.

Boba's family, which did not live far from Rani's family, was very different from Rani's family. His father, Tathaji, a self-made person, was a teetotaller and an educationist. Boba's mother would not generally keep good health. Tathaji worked passionately for nearly 20 hours every day and had a transferable government teaching job. Due to his father's constant absence from home, Boba proactively helped his mother in raising her young family and in her daily chores around the house

In 1961, Boba completed his first undergraduate degree, BA, with double course Mathematics and Physics as his major subjects. He scored third position in Jammu & Kashmir University. At that time, his father, Tathaji, was posted as the Headmaster, Government High School, Leh, in Ladakh. Boba's elder sister, Behanji, was also away from home at Banihal, where she was posted as the second mistress in a government girls' school. During that period, Boba constantly took care of his ailing mother, Amaji, and his two younger sisters, Phoola and Basanti, who were both students at a local girls' school.

In his father's absence, Boba was the man of the house for a significant period. It is said that, during his final year of BA at Amar Singh College, Srinagar, Boba would cook and clean the house, located at Alikadal, in downtown Srinagar, before leaving for college. Once it so happened that due to extreme bad weather conditions, Tathaji's money order from Leh did not reach home for a number of weeks. In order to meet the daily living expenses of the home, Boba tutored a number of primary and high school students, with good results. In the process, he also discovered his passion for teaching, just like his father.

Those days, Amaji would remain ill for most of the time. She was referred to Dr Thusoo, a famous physician in Srinagar at that time, who reportedly advised the family that she had less than six months to live. She was obviously devastated to hear this, as were the other family members. Before her death, she desperately wanted to see Boba married off. Suddenly, in the Alikadal home, the focus had shifted from Amaji's sickness to Boba's wedding. It is noteworthy that before Behanji's birth,

Amaji had lost four male children one after the other. Of her four surviving children, Boba was the only male child and enjoyed a special place in her eyes.

Behanji was fond of Rani, whom she had first seen in the neighbourhood of her maternal (Kadalbajoo) home. Rani's family and the Kadalbajoos were neighbours at Gurgari Mohalla, Alikadal. Behanji facilitated a meeting between Amaji and Kaki at Reshpeer Sahib's shrine in Alikadal, following which the two mothers locked the engagement.

**Married Teenagers**

Rani and Boba were unique in their own ways; both were young and gifted in their own ways; both constantly supported their mothers and other siblings. In both families, fathers remained busy with work and lived away from home for extended periods of time.

In June 1961, they were engaged to marry. Rani's family lived in the neighbourhood of Amaji's parental home. The wedding was scheduled in November 1961.

At the time of his engagement, Boba had just completed his BA, securing third position in the Jammu & Kashmir state. He had majored in Mathematics (double course) and Physics. With his strong background in Mathematics, he wanted to make a career in statistics, primarily driven by the reason that the starting salary of a statistician, in Delhi, at that time was around Rupees 700 per month, which was more than what Tathaji was earning at that time despite being a gazetted officer.

So, one day, Boba visited Kashmir University to explore the possibility of his admission to undertake further studies in statistics. There he met Professor Jan Mohammad, the Head of Department of Mathematics, who assured him that he would easily secure admission to Master's Degree in Statistics. However, Professor Mohammad strongly encouraged him to approach Public Service Commission and seek admission in an engineering college for pursuing an engineering career instead. With this guidance, Boba applied to PSC for admission into an engineering college. Professor Mohammad's advice had also coincided with advice from Behanji, his older sister, who had also been persuading him to study engineering.

Between June and August 1961, Boba received admission telegrams from two reputed universities, Banaras Hindu University (BHU) and Ranchi Engineering College. However, due to his love for Kashmir and reluctance to leave the valley, he hid both these telegrams under a carpet.

As destiny would have it, on 4 August 1961, as he was having a siesta in the afternoon, he heard someone ringing a bell at the front gate of the house and shouting his name in the process. Boba got up and had a look from his fourth storey balcony. He saw a tall uniformed peon from the government, wearing a big turban, with a colourful tora at the top, loudly calling his name. He hurriedly went downstairs to meet the peon. To his dismay, he was informed that he had been nominated for admission to Punjab Engineering College (PEC), Chandigarh. He was also handed a sealed envelope. This time, however, Boba could not hide the letter, as his mother and the neighbours had witnessed the scene. Due to anxiety and stress, he had a bout of fever. He really did not want to go away from Kashmir. A relative, Jia Lal Tiku sahib, acted firmly in the absence of Tathaji. Tiku sahib brought a doctor to see Boba at home. He also made all the necessary arrangements for Boba's travel to Chandigarh.

Boba arrived at PEC on 17 August 1961, late by more than two weeks, as the session had started on 1 August 1961. The college principal, Dr P N Khanna, was not very happy. Boba pleaded strongly, providing the reasons for his late arrival. Upon that, the principal gave him a provisional admission on the condition that he had to make up for the lost time and secure good grades, which he did without much effort, given that he had performed so well in his earlier undergraduate degree.

In the next three months, Boba studied hard and performed very well in his studies. He also realised that he needed to focus fully on his studies and perhaps it was not a good idea for him to marry at that stage of his life. Four days prior to the scheduled wedding day in November 1961, Boba sat alone in the evening under a tree at the college football oval, not far from his hostel block, and cried bitterly. He had almost decided not to go ahead with the wedding. After all, he was just 18-years-old. Under emotional compulsions, his unquestionable obedience to his parents, and deep love and care for his mother, Boba decided to comply with his mother's wish, without a question.

On reaching home two days before his wedding, he wrote, *tragedy—11 November 1961* with chalk on a smoke darkened timber beam in the house attic.

Boba and Rani were married on 11 November 1961. He left for Chandigarh a few days later. In all, they had just about one week to see and know each other after their wedding day. Could they have fallen in love with each other? Did they discover soul mates in each other?

After Boba's return to Chandigarh, Rani was left on her own, living in the company of Boba's mother and his sisters, although her family did not live very far away. She could not communicate with her husband for months together. Mobile phones did not exist those days. How did they communicate without feeling any need for any verbal or written communication with each other? Life must not have been easy for the two young hearts. Boba would look for every opportunity to visit his home and see Rani. He would sneak away quite often from college and visit Srinagar, in particular around common festivals and public holidays.

## Billu

In August 1962, nine months after her wedding, Rani delivered through a caesarean section, a healthy male baby. The baby was named Billu by Tathaji and Gitton by Pitaji, the other grandpa.

During those initial days at the hospital, it is said, some Caucasian Catholic nuns, visiting the hospital on one of those days, had baptised Billu, much to the ignorance of the mother. Interestingly, Billu had also been fed *aab-e-zum zum*, the sacred water from Saudi Arabia, which was brought by a family member of another new mother lying on the adjacent bed.

Billu had thus been fed with sacred drops of water from both the Muslim and Catholic communities soon after his birth. Did these sacred drops of water prove to be significant in shaping Billu's personality and outlook in his adult life? Global Initiation.

Boba successfully obtained his BSc Engineering degree in 1965 and returned home. Billu was three years old at that time. Billu has no memories from his first three years. Interestingly, Rani and Boba, both being fairly young, were not able to exercise complete freedom to keep their baby in their lap or hug or cuddle him in the presence of other family members. It is also said that Boba would not even shave his beard in the presence of Tathaji. In such an environment, Billu was mainly brought up by Amaji, with support from Rani, and Boba's younger sisters, Auntie and Didi, who are about seven and four years younger than Boba.

## The Koul home

Billu spent his initial years mostly in the company of his grandmother and aunts. Rani was inhibited in performing her role as his mother, as she was considered to be too young by Boba's family to be called his mother. Perhaps Billu was considered mainly as a part of Boba and, with that, his grandmother and aunts claimed ownership. They did everything to raise him as their own.

Deep inside, however, Billu had a very close bond with Rani who, whenever she had the opportunity, away from the eyes of others, held him in her lap. He felt safe. After all, he had been a physical part of her for those nine months. She was his soul mate. Deep inside, he also knew his biological relationship with Boba during his early years, although they did not see each other much before Boba returned from Chandigarh. Like Rani, Boba also had inhibitions in openly accepting his relationship with Billu.

Rani did not have any direct income. For the first three years after her wedding, she depended solely on doles from her own family and, to some lesser extent, on Boba's family. Her father-in-law, Tathaji, did try to encourage her to pursue her education and have a career of her own, but she had shown no particular enthusiasm and interest in doing so. After Boba's return, she started receiving an occasional dole from her husband, although he would still shy away from her in front of his family members.

Rani always knew what Billu wanted. How did they communicate? Perhaps she was the only one in the world who had such unconditional and uninhibited love for him. She would listen to him, although he would not speak much those days. She never tried to cut him off or impose her thoughts on him. She would read to him when others would not be looking. This helped him to develop an open and independent mind, with critical thinking.

Despite her limited access to money, Rani somehow managed to provide most indoor games of the time and common outdoor sports equipment to Billu, obviously from her own savings. He had everything that a child could have but he did not have a mate to play with in his own home. He had no cousins and no siblings to play with. Rani was medically not capable of producing another child. During his early years, the relationship between his parents was quite tumultuous, much to his alarm. With a generally chaotic environment at home, he suffered from severe mental stress. However, as he grew, the relationship between his parents started getting relatively normalised, in particular after Behanji married Abujan is 1970, followed by the wedding of his aunts, Auntie and Didi, in October 1971. With time, Rani's focus gradually shifted from Billu to Boba, with an attempt to regain the essence of all those past years and restore her relationship to where it should have been in the beginning. And she was justified as a human being. She wanted to salvage all those lost years.

**Tathaji**

Tathaji, Billu's paternal grandfather, was born in 1908 in Srinagar. His father Pandit Sona Koul, a self-made man, was a banker by profession but a saintly person by nature. At a very young age, Tathaji lost his biological mother, Richhmaal, and was brought up mainly by his aunt, Yemberzel, who was a widow. His step-mother also loved him dearly.

From an early age, he was inclined to reading books and was, therefore, quite bright in his studies. All through his student life, he received numerous scholarships from his school. In his own words, on the annual school day after his Year 8 Board Examination, he had received 11 prizes in one session from the hands of Maharaja Sir Partap Singh, who could not hide an increasingly curious look at Tathaji's face every time when his name was called to come to the dais and receive a prize.

He had started earning his pocket money from the age of 12 through private tutoring of other students, thereby becoming less reliant on his father's dole.

After the completion of Bachelor's degree in Arts, with major in Mathematics, he was offered a teaching position at Hanfia Institute at Anantnag, which he served for nearly 21 years, initially as a teacher and subsequently as Headmaster. Thereafter, Tathaji served as Headmaster in various high schools at Leh (Ladakh) and across the valley (Rangteng, Bandpore, Khrew, Bumai) and at Sri Ranbir High School, Jammu. For the exemplary services rendered by him at Leh, he received commendations and awards from Pandit Jawaharlal Nehru (the first Prime Minister of India) and Karan Singh (then Sadr-i-Riyasat).

Tathaji was a very popular and well respected high school mathematics teacher in the valley. Due to his love for Anantnag and its people, he maintained his post office pass book account there after his transfer to Jammu in the mid-fifties. In the seventies, he visited Anantnag almost on a monthly basis and Billu accompanied him several times. The common people of Anantnag, particularly from the Muslim community, would greet him with a warm hug. Interestingly, it would take them nearly two hours to foot a mile long distance between Nagbal and the Anantnag bus stand. After every 50 feet or so, someone would greet and hug him and engage him in a warm chat for a few minutes.

Syed Mir Qasim, a former J&K chief minister was one of his illustrious students, as were several members of the influential Kochak family of Anantnag. His popularity amongst the Muslim and other non-Pandit communities (eg. Dogra, Ladakhi and Punjabis) was a result of his selfless service, which he rendered with sincerity and without any bias or discrimination based on religion or ethnicity.

Tathaji had strong interest in English literature (Shakespearean plays) and psychology. He was also an ardent sportsman in his younger days. He liked swimming and played cricket as a fast bowler, and football. He generally spoke in fluent English at home and, in particular, with Billu.

His personal deity was the Mother Goddess. On a regular basis, he would chant all five chapters of *Panchastavi*, which are hymns in Sanskrit in the praise of the Mother Goddess. He did not believe in formal religious rituals. He would visit various shrines, *Ksheer Bhawani* at Tulmul, *Jawala Devi* at Khrew and *Jaesta Mata* in Srinagar but only on working days of a week when not many people would be expected to be there. He would spend most of the time there in full recitation of *Panchastavi*.

Tathaji had written a text book on English Grammar during his stint at Sri Ranbir High School, Jammu, in the fifties. Billu had salvaged a copy of the book and saved it with his important papers at his Rawalpora house. Unfortunately, that book was also lost along with all other family treasures when the Koul family left Kashmir in January 1990.

Tathaji did not inherit any wealth or family artefacts from his father. When his father, Pandit Sona Koul, passed away suddenly in Srinagar, Tathaji was at Anantnag. Family stories say, his close relatives had overnight transported his father's safe, full of gold and silver ornaments, in a *shikara* (a boat) to a friend' house at Habba Kadal. The family pashmina was also taken away. They had not even spared Tathaji's treasure of books, which he had won through numerous scholarships over his schooling years. The books were sold to a local grocer by weight. A few days after his father's demise, when he bought something from that grocer, he saw the grocer cutting a page from one of his books for packing purposes. Tathaji asked the grocer about the source of that book and the grocer told him the entire story. Although many books had been consumed by the grocer, Tathaji still managed to buy back some of the remaining books but only after paying the actual costs of the books.

Tathaji did not stop working upon his retirement from government services in 1963. He continued working, first at Vishwa Bharti College, Rainawari, and subsequently at Vidhya Bhawan High School, Nawakadal, Srinagar, till his sudden death on 12 January 1983. He died silently and peacefully in his chair, halfway during his meals, due to a sudden massive heart attack.

**Vegetarian**

*I am an ant which is trodden under foot,*
*Not that wasp, the pain of whose sting causes lament.*
*How shall I give due thanks for the blessing*
*That I do not possess the strength of injuring mankind?*

—Sa'di
Gulistan

It is said Boba had been very ill during his childhood, somewhere in late 1940s or early 1950s. For his speedy and full recovery, on somebody's advice, Amaji had promised to perform the sacrifice of a lamb, as may have been a common practice in Kashmir those days. The ritual was called *Raazkath*. Due to Tathaji transferable job, the family had to spend a number of years in Jammu, before returning to Srinagar in 1959 when Tathaji was transferred to Ladakh. For these and other reasons, Amaji had not been able to fulfil her promise till Boba returned from Chandigarh.

Upon being reminded, the sacrificial ceremony of *Raazkath* was performed at a cremation ground in Anantnag, in Southern Kashmir, on an autumn day in 1965. Billu remembers that day very well and how he had walked with Tathaji, holding his hand, on a long earthen embankment. Billu remembers seeing a red object hanging by a tree from a distance upon which he asked Tathaji if the red object was Auntie's sweater, as he had previously seen her wearing a red sweater. Perhaps Tathaji said nothing. On reaching nearer to the tree, he observed red blood dripping from a skinned-off sheep. It was a traumatic experience for Billu, a part of him died instantaneously. He became afraid of humans; they appeared to be so cruel. Why did they kill the poor sheep? That day he lost some faith in mankind.

As per the ritual, the body of the poor sheep was cut into small chunks, which were fried and then served to people in earthen bowl-shaped plates. Nearly 30 people, mainly the members of his extended family and friends, were present to attend the ritual. He could not even look at his plate and kicked it down the embankment slope in anger and disgust. He had made a shocking discovery that the meat that people commonly cooked and consumed, was sourced from a sheep's body.

The family did not treat him as a natural vegetarian till he was about ten years old. Although the *Raazkath* event turned Billu away from meat consumption, he continued to consume fish and dried fish dishes during his first ten years. He never ate chicken though. On a daily basis, however, as most meat dishes were with vegetables, his meal generally comprised rice, which is the staple cereal of Kashmiris, with vegetables, without the meat pieces.

This practice continued till he was about 12 year old. However, one day during the winter months of 1974, Tathaji said that new born babies who die after birth are consigned to a watery grave where the fish eat them. On hearing this, Billu immediately announced that he would no longer consume any fish or fish products. He also announced that he would no longer consume vegetables that were cooked with meat or fish.

Some incidents related to Billu's vegetarian food preference are noteworthy. The first one happened when Billu would have been about 11 year old, on a summer day in 1973, when Billu was made to swallow a whole meat ball, after being asked to eat that meat ball by Auntie's husband. Auntie was married to a Kashmiri businessman.

Auntie would visit Kashmir every summer for a couple of months. Uncle Ashok would join her for a week or so towards the end. Uncle Ashok, despite being of Kashmiri origin, did not look like a Kashmiri. Billu was very afraid of Uncle Ashok. One day, while eating lunch, Uncle Ashok asked Billu to eat a minced meat ball.

The second incident happened when Billu was about 13 year old. During his winter break, in January 1976, after his Year 9 final examination, Billu spent a few weeks with his maternal grandmother, Kaki, and Boba Maama. Both loved him very much. One day, Billu found a small splinter of bone in his vegetarian dish. He guessed that Kaki would have cooked meat and vegetables together, but served them separately. With that, he completely lost his mind and abused his grandmother, only to repent later. Words can't be taken back; some spoken words haunt people all their life. He never forgave himself for shouting at his grandmother who loved him so much. It would have been out of her deep love and care for him that she would have cooked the two together so that he received some additional nutrition.

In his childhood, as well in his adulthood, Billu experienced numerous embarrassing moments in social settings for being a vegetarian. Interestingly, the loathing villain was always a fellow Kashmiri Pandit. He often wondered why only Pandits had scoffed at him and harassed him for being a vegetarian.

In circa 1974, in a *Mehandiraat* dinner, a cousin requested all *vaishnavs* (meaning the vegetarians) to move to one corner of the *shamiana* (canopy) for ease in service. Those days, the guests used to be served while sitting on the floor. On hearing the announcement, Billu stood up and moved to the designated corner. On spotting him amongst the group of vegetarians, the host sarcastically shouted from his corner, 'Billuji, are you also a *vaishnav*? You father eats meat every day.' After that day, Billu did not eat at any wedding for the next four years or so.

Another incident took place in January 1991 in Jammu. His father-in-law's friend, an old resident of Jammu, invited him for dinner. Rekha could not go; she was still recuperating after Deeksha's caesarean childbirth. Billu was taken home by the host's son. To start with, Billu was served with oranges and tea with biscuits, however, all other guests and the host had fried fish and chicken, with alcoholic drinks. The main meal was served as buffet. Several large bowls, containing non-vegetarian dishes, lined one longer side of the dining table. On the opposite longer side, four small bowls, containing vegetarian food, were placed close to one another in a cluster formation. Due to the arrangements of the bowls, Billu found himself alone on one side of the table whereas the host and the three other families ate and chatted on the other side. On noticing this, a gentleman crossed over to Billu's side to give him company. On seeing that, the host shouted, '*Mahara*, don't go there. You'll get polluted.' On hearing this, Billu's first instinct was to place his plate on the table and walk out, but somehow he managed to control himself, gulped down a glass of water and finished his meal. He suffered silently that evening till he was dropped back at his home late in the night.

After leaving India, Billu and his family have been hosted warmly by many people from different ethnic and religious backgrounds, which include Malaysians, both Chinese and Malays; Indonesians; Pakistani Muslims; people of Bahai faith; and Catholic white Australians. All have prepared full vegetarian cuisine and have respected his food preference. It is in his own community that he found resistance.

## Boba Maama

Billu's maternal grandmother, Kaki, and his maternal uncle, Boba Maama, played a very significant part in his early upbringing. His father (Boba) was mainly away during the first three years of his life and because of the tumultuous relationship between his parents upon his father's return from Chandigarh, it was Boba Maama who had assumed a father's role during those early years of his life.

Billu has a very hazy memory about his maternal grandfather, Pitaji, who passed away when he would have been about three years old.

During his early childhood, around the age of 2 or 3 years, Billu had an attack of chicken pox. As Boba was away at Chandigarh at that time, Rani had moved to her mother's home for a few months. Boba Maama would carry him in his lap most of the time. One day, as he was eating his lunch, Billu pissed and some drops fell in Boba Maama's plate. Instead of discarding the plate, he had calmly pushed aside the contaminated food and continued to eat from the same plate. Typical Boba Maama. Totally unflappable.

Boba Maama was a very intelligent person, with a range of skills which not many people had those days. He was a philatelist, with a huge collection of rare stamps, neatly secured in a number of albums. Perhaps he was not aware his stamp collection was worth a fortune in the international market. Unfortunately, the stamp albums were left behind when he and his family suddenly left Kashmir after 1990.

He was a keen photographer. He had a Yashica box camera. If not for him and his interest in photography, all those black and white photographs from Billu's childhood would not exist. He knew a great deal about origami. He taught Billu how to make a range of paper toys and various figures.

He was also a great storyteller. He would lie down, close his eyes, pretend to be fast asleep and soon start murmuring a story, as if he was dreaming. The story would be usually about a fairy (*pari*). Amazingly, it would always be a new story every time. The stories were engaging and logical. He would have been a popular story writer, had he chosen to publish them. Like Rani, he also had a good voice. He generally sang sad Hindi film songs, originally sung by Mukesh.

It was Boba Maama who introduced basic arithmetic to Billu. He also taught him how to play chess, carom and so many other board games.

## Summer of 1967

Billu had long and uncut curly light brown hair until the age of about 5 years. In Rani's own words, he had golden brown hair. After combing his hair daily, she would weave his hair in two plaits and then tie them at the top of his head, similar to the Sikh kids. This could have been a time-consuming daily chore for Rani. Boba, who mostly lived at Baramulla, was busy constructing a new government hospital building. From time to time, Auntie, Didi and Amaji would visit him for a few days, as would many other relatives. Billu would also accompany his grandmother and aunts; however, Rani would never be with them.

In September 1967, Rani had suddenly returned to her mother's home after possibly having a serious dispute with her in-laws. She was a young intelligent woman, who also had dreams. Though very clear hearted, being young, she would have been outspoken to an extent, much to the annoyance of her orthodox, rather naive and backward-thinking, women in-laws. Like any other young housewife, she would definitely have wanted to be with her husband at Baramulla, but due to the outdated family values, ridiculous to be precise, and sickening politics within the broader Koul family, she was forbidden to do so.

With Rani's sudden return to her mother's home, it would have been understandably difficult for Amaji to look after Billu. One day, in August 1967, she took him to the Ksheer Bhawani shrine at Tulmul, where his *zarkasay* ceremony was performed. His long golden locks were buried in the ground along with some walnuts. He was told that a walnut tree will grow at the spot. Soon after his *zarkasay*, they visited Boba and stayed at his Baramulla government quarter for a few days.

Boba's two-storey government residential quarter at Khoja Bagh faced a beautiful hill. Several poppy fields lay between the quarter and the hill. Boba's domestic helper would pick young lambs from the fields in his lap and bring them home for Billu to play with. After Boba would leave for work, Billu would sit alone for hours in the sun on the backside verandah that led to a kitchen garden. He would pick up lumps of moist clayey soil from the garden beds and keenly mould them into several geometrical shapes, such as cubes, pyramids, spheres, wheels, cylinders etc. of different sizes and leave them to dry in the sun on the plinth projection. Little did he know that he would be engineering the same soil as an adult.

The quarter had a large second storey balcony facing the hill where Boba and others would sit most evenings, listen to Mohd Rafi's songs on his transistor and sing along. Sometimes they watched the moon. Billu would silently just soak in the whole environment. It was a beautiful setting on the whole, but his mother was missing from the scene. Billu missed his mother.

On some afternoons, Boba played badminton with other government officers who lived nearby. He would also play cards with his friends on Sundays. Boba would usually take Billu out with him when he would go to the market to buy vegetables and meat from Pattan; Das Ram would do most of the grocery shopping. Boba seemed to walk very fast and Billu would have to run after him to keep up. They also watched a couple of Hindi movies at a cinema hall in the Baramulla town, one was *Raaz* and the other one was *Aaakhri Khat*, both starring legendary Rajesh Khanna. Billu cried while watching both these movies. He also felt claustrophobic in the cinema hall.

One late sunny morning, Billu was alone in the upstairs balcony, looking at the hill and the beautiful red popy flowers in the field at its foothill. Amaji and his aunts were downstairs. Suddenly, he heard some commotion in the front yard of the house. A large number of people seemed to have gathered there. Someone shouted from downstairs, 'Billu, close your door and hide yourself.' Billu did what he was ordered to do.

After a few minutes, he heard someone knocking at his door, but he did not open it. Suddenly, the window pane adjacent to the door got smashed and a hand entered and opened the door latch. When the door opened, he saw his maternal uncle, Boba Maama (whom he called 'Bua' at that time) standing in the doorway. Boba Maama wore a light lemon coloured bush shirt, white trousers and white shoes. For reassuring Billu, he said, 'Gittonji, I have come to take you back to your mother. She is waiting for you outside in the car. Just remain calm. Don't worry and don't be afraid of anyone.'

However, Billu started crying and shouted for Amaji. Upon this, Boba Maama picked him up and hurried downstairs. Billu kept crying for Amaji and shouted to his uncle, 'Leave me, I want to go to Amaji.' Outside the house, nearly a hundred people had assembled. Even after meeting his mother in the waiting car, he continued to cry and requested to be taken back to Amaji. Rani hugged and kissed him, with tears flowing but he did not feel very comfortable.

Billu's maternal family lived at Sathu-barbarshah at that time. A couple of hours later, he was comforted by Kaki when he reached his maternal home. Kaki was so fair, beautiful and soft, like an angel. Rani stuck to him closely. She and her brother tried everything to comfort Billu with hugs and kisses and his favourite toys. With all the love from his mother and her family, Billu recovered from his traumatic experience within a few days. A few weeks later, when Rani (teasingly) told him that he was being sent back to Amaji, Billu refused to go.

Billu lived for nearly two years with his maternal family. His uncle earnestly took over the role of a disciplinary father and tutored him daily at home. Although he was very stern during the tutoring sessions and a hard task master, Boba Maama also played a number of board games with him in the evenings. He also taught him how to make a number of paper toys. Rani and Kaki pampered him in their own ways.

He would play with kids in the neighbourhood and Kaki would always remain very tense when he would go out to play due to a serious concern for his safety. In fact, in late January 1969, she hid away his favourite 3-feet long toy gun, which had a wooden baton, while he was taking lunch one day. He and his toy gun were inseparable. On that day, he had placed his toy gun behind him while eating lunch facing a window. After finishing, when he turned around, the gun was missing. He wailed and pleaded with Kaki to return it to him. She pretended complete ignorance and guessed aloud, possibly the *gar-devta* (the resident God) may have taken it. He half-believed it.

During his stay at his maternal home, he sleepwalked during some nights. One night, after climbing down two flight of stairs and just when he was about to open the latch on the front door of the house, he was pulled back by Rani. Concerned with his sleeping disorder, she took him to Lallaji, a visually challenged local saint. Lallaji placed his right hand gently on his head, whispered some mantra, and applied some ashes (from daily prayers) on his head. Billu never walked again in his sleep.

In the winter of 1968/1969, he suffered an attack of jaundice. He remained bedridden for about a month.

By March 1969, following an agreement in the background between the two families, Rani and Billu returned to their home after a period of nearly a year and a half. An overarching factor in her decision had been her love for her husband. Her dispute with her in-laws was mainly driven by her desire to be with him and their resistance to allow that to happen.

In the summer 1969, the family went for a 2-week long vacation to Gulmarg and Tangmarg. It was a fun filled outing; Billu's first one in years. He loved the lush green meadows of Gulmarg and the brook at Tangmarg. He was absolutely at peace with nature and himself, such as never before.

During this trip, he found his mother remarkably happy for the first time. They stayed at a luxurious Forest Department hut at Tangmarg and then moved to a Tourist hut at Gulmarg. One day, Billu discovered the healing power of Iodex, which had miraculously helped him to recover within a couple of hours from a crippling muscle sprain which had bothered him for almost a day.

A week after returning from the trip, Billu was admitted to Vidhya Bhavan School, at Bhatyaar. After his initial assessment by the school, he was made to sit directly in Year 3. He was seven year old at that time. Due to Boba Maama's careful tutoring, he stood third in his class in the six-monthly examination held in September 1969. Thereafter, it was all downhill.

From March 1970 onwards, Year 4 was no different than the later part of Year 3. His reading and written English skills had become subpar, in fact absolutely poor, although his spoken English was reasonably fine, courtesy Tathaji, who generally spoke in English. Unbelievably, at the age of eight, he did not know how to read time on a wrist watch.

In short, Billu struggled in his studies mainly because he could just not learn by rote. At school, due to his general inability to complete homework, he frequently got punished by his class teachers. They would use a bamboo cane to hit the palms of defaulting students, as well on their buttocks sometimes to humiliate them. Some teachers would resort to Murga, a demeaning squatting posture, as punishment. He never complained at home; who would listen? Due to his recurring poor performance in spot tests at home, he was humiliated and grounded from playing outside. He struggled to find a solution.

Although on surface, to an external eye, things seemed to be normal at home, but the disturbing undercurrents in the family were not hidden to Billu. He was an extremely sensitive boy; very observant but quiet. The distracting home environment significantly affected his retention and focus on studies. He was not a very happy boy inside. Internally, he constantly suffered for his mother, who was not a very happy woman either. At times, his mother would physically get assaulted, yet she endured, most possibly for his future. He never reacted or said anything to anyone, as that would have certainly jeopardised Rani's sacrifice. She remained resolute and defiant but never left her home again, despite serious provocations from the family. At times, she would go without food for days. On those occasions, her mother would send food for her through some common acquaintance. In such an unhealthy environment, how long could a child like Billu survive? Something had to change! It did later that year in October 1970.

## Behanji's marriage

Just days before the Deepavali festival in October 1970, there was commotion of some kind in the family. Billu and his younger two aunts were suddenly moved, in a hushed move and under the cover of darkness, to Bal Garden where Benigashi lived with her family. Amaji was moved to Habba Kadal where Bhaigash and his wife lived. Why? Because, Behanji had married her long-term boyfriend, Mufti Nazir Ahmad (*Abujan*). The family expected a massive reaction, possibly an onslaught, from the angry Pandit community.

At Benigashi's (Amaji's sister) home, Billu was quiet and observant as usual, but emotionally very diffused and flabbergasted. On the evening of Deepavali, he asked for firecrackers. Auntie slapped him but Papaji (granduncle) admonished her. He loved Billu. In the past, whenever Billu had visited Benigashi's home with Amaji, Papaji would hold his hand and make him sit with him for hours together. Benigashi's family were some kind of reformists and would traditionally not burn firecrackers. However, that evening, Papaji broke that rule for Billu, he bought him a bag full of firecrackers and sparklers. As Billu could not burn most of them, Kukuji jumped in and excitedly took over. By default, he had received a rare opportunity to celebrate Deepavali like the other kids in the neighbourhood.

A month later, in November 1970, Benigashi helped the Kouls in finding accommodation in the nearby colony of Narsingh Garh. In the meantime, Billu's aunt, Phoolaji (*Didi*) went to Jammu to study law at Jammu University.

After moving to Narsing Garh, Billu was admitted to Year 4 at Vidhya Niketan School, at Karan Nagar. The classroom strength was nearly half of his previous classroom at Vidhya Bhavan School. In his new school, therefore, he was seated much closer to the teacher and the blackboard. In his new school, students sat on benches instead of a jute-matted floor. Boba worked very hard with him during the next three months to enable him to pass his final examinations in March 1971. On occasions, when he would fail the spot tests, Boba sarcastically called him a *shining star*.

From 1971 onwards, in his Year 5 class, Billu started to gain a gradual focus on his studies, despite spending a considerable amount of time playing cricket and marbles with kids in the neighbourhood. His reading and written English skills were still subpar. He was still not able to learn by rote. Although he had not been able to memorise tables after 11, he had found a way to arrive at the answer. He could still not read time on a wrist watch. As time passed, his confidence and comfort levels gradually grew.

The family environment was relatively much more peaceful and quieter than before. Boba was transferred to the Design Directorate in Srinagar; he would return home early after work. That addressed Rani's issues. The couple had started to bond. Billu's distractions were fading one by one. Over the year, as peace grew in the home, his emotional world stabilised considerably.

In October 1971, just before Deepavali, Auntie and Didi were married off on the same day. Billu's *mekhal* ceremony was also performed during the wedding days.

On the wedding day, the house was beautifully decorated with colourful lights. A large decorated canopy was installed outside on the street for receiving and entertaining the guests. The members of the Delhi *barat* (groom's wedding procession) spent a considerably long time in showing off their dancing skills, many of them had a red coloured *paan* drool oozing from their mouth. Interestingly, they were made to pay for their dancing adventure. As they danced, nearly 600 members of the Rainawari *barat* consumed most of the (meat based) food that had been prepared for the two *barats*. As a result, Boba had to organise additional meat supplies at a very short notice, which took a considerable time to cook. The 50 odd members of the Delhi *barat* were made to wait before being served; it seemed they had been punished (by the Rainawari people) for dancing. First come, first served!

As a first in Srinagar, espresso coffee had been served to guests. Several eyewitnesses reported that many guests and relatives had deliberately dropped their empty (china) cups on the pavement to break them after consuming coffee, showing their sadistic side. Boba had to pay a considerable amount for the loss of a large number of coffee cups.

After his elder sister had married a Muslim, Boba faced a lot of criticism and aggressive behaviour from members of the Pandit community. He also faced comments from his Muslim friends and colleagues. He could not hide from the world, howsoever hard he wished to. He was not sure about the two younger sisters, especially the middle sister who was studying law at Jammu. He had no guarantee whatsoever that his sisters would not follow their eldest sister and marry outside the Pandit community. His parents would have also been exposed to similar aggression from the wider Kashmiri community. All members of the family were taunted by people for a number of years. Even Billu was not spared by many kids at his school and in the neighbourhood.

After the weddings, the family was reduced to just five people—Billu, his parents and his grandparents. It was a much quieter home now; Rani and Billu had much more time for each other and for interaction with Boba. For the first time, Billu was beginning to have a feel of a regular family structure.

One day while playing outside with the kids, Billu had a fight with the son of a neighbour, who regularly borrowed sugar, oil, rice etc. from Rani. Billu teased him, saying, 'Hey

hey, aren't you the one who borrows everything from my mother?' Rani overheard him saying this. She came out quickly, carrying Tathaji's Bata leather sandal in her hand and severely beat him. He cried a lot with pain and subsequently developed fever. Later in life, he felt very grateful to his mother for giving him a timely lesson. Rani was an extremely benevolent person. She had herself experienced severe hardships from time to time in her earlier life. As a result of those hardships, she had developed a very helpful attitude. She seemed to have clearly understood what it took to borrow things from other people. Therefore, she never returned any needy person empty handed. She showed a great deal of empathy and humility towards other sufferers. She never mentioned her helpful acts to anyone, not even to herself.

Billu took his final Year 5 examinations in November 1971. This was the first time when the final school examinations had moved from March to November in Srinagar. The new school year started immediately after the results were announced. He passed his Year 5 examinations and moved to Year 6.

The historical Indo-Pak war broke out on 3 December 1971 and lasted for about 13 days before ending suddenly on 16 December 1971. During the war, war sirens and blackouts were regular features. Extreme fear loomed in the air. Billu witnessed a couple of dogfights in the sky between the fighter planes of the two countries.

Rani subscribed to a Hindi magazine called *Dharamyug*, from which he learnt the names of fighter planes of both India and Pakistan, as well as the names of the naval ships. Rani inspired him with true stories of valour and gallantry shown by the Indian soldiers in that war and in the previous wars. She said the Indian soldiers always repel the invader and always march ahead despite being shot; they always rise to their feet even when they fall; they never give up or take a backward step, and finally when they die in the battlefield they fall on their front and never on their back. Inspired by his mother, he too wanted to be a soldier. Little did he know at that age that his life would be nothing but a battlefield and he had to soldier on till the end.

Rani read a lot of literature and subscribed to a number of magazines. When she was not busy doing household chores, she would either knit or read her books. She had a very keen interest in history.

**School Years**

In March 1972, Billu returned to his school with new found zeal and a greater focus. Fortunately, he liked all his teachers and the way they taught in the class. During the winter break of 1971-72, he thought really long and hard as to why he had not been able to do well in the school in the past. He realised that only his knowledge would serve him in the good stead. With his parents' relationship stabilised, all he wanted in the world was to acquire an ability to understand what the teachers taught in the class and then be able to reproduce that. He also realised that there was no greater happiness for him in the world than being the top student of his class. His world had been dark in the past and he wanted it to be lit.

He accepted that he did not have the ability to undertake rote learning; this method was simply not meant for him. His only option was to really *understand* the basic concepts of what was taught at the school and work on those concepts on a daily basis at home. During those long winter nights in the bed, he thoroughly analysed his strengths and weaknesses. Amongst his weaknesses were (a) his natural body clock, which was responsible for his tendency to fall asleep around 8 pm, at least three to four hours before the remaining members of his family; and (b) his inability to use rote learning. Paradoxically, these very factors were also his strengths. Because he would sleep early, he would also wake up naturally very early the next morning, with a fresher body and mind. Also, his inability to rote had forced him to resort to conceptual understanding of the subject matter, which had the potential to result in lifelong learning. Between the two scenarios, he found himself actually in a relatively more advantageous situation.

On the back of his deep contemplation and self-assessment during that winter, he returned to the school in March 1972 with a plan. On the very first day of the school, he moved to the front of the class. He also used a portion of his lunch break in doing a part of his homework. On reaching home, he finished his school work first before going out to play. Luckily, he had always been an early riser, so he did not need to be woken up or rely on an alarm clock to wake up early. Next morning, when he woke up as usual, around 4.30 am, he first looked at the picture of Goddess Sarasvati on a large photo calendar that hung on the wall opposite to his bed. He prayed to her to unlock his wisdom chamber and let his intelligence flow into his brain. Thereafter, he sat in his bed and revised everything that had been taught at the school the day before. So, when he went to school, he was better prepared for the day and felt very confident.

His confidence paid off. It was the start of an upward spiral. Soon, in his weekly and monthly class tests, he started standing second and third in the class. The first position holder was always Sanjay Bhan.

One cloudy afternoon of November 1972, the school assembled for the results of the final examinations. Billu stood with his classmates. Suddenly, he heard his Form Teacher asking someone, 'Where is my first position holder?' The students turned around to face her. As soon as she saw Billu, she exclaimed, 'Ah, there he is!' He could not believe it. He looked around to confirm if it was really him or someone else.

His Form Teacher motioned for him to come forward and stand near her. His name was announced as the first position holder of Year 6 class. He was simply spellbound. A miracle had indeed happened.

Vidhya Niketan School provided schooling only up to Year 6 at that time. He had to look for a new school. After undertaking some research about schools, Boba chose DAV Institute, at Jawahar Nagar, for Billu's admission to Year 7.

After his resurrection a few months ago, he entered his new school, in March 1973 with a great deal of confidence.

In October that year, eleven-year-old Billu was left alone with his 68-year-old grandfather to look after himself in the harsh late autumn weather of Kashmir. With winter fast approaching, between the two of them, they had to attend to their respective schools, and also look after their food and various household chores. After the school, Tathaji remained busy with tuitions and returned home by midnight. Billu returned from school by 4.30 pm in his school bus. He would stay alone for up to six hours every night, sometimes without power due to frequent power outages. He spent many nights studying under a lantern before falling asleep over his books and notebooks.

Tathaji had some basic cooking skills. Billu learnt how to clean uncooked rice and cook it. On a regular basis, during those two months and a bit, he washed clothes, cleaned the floor with a broom, cut the vegetables and, in his spare time, completed his homework, before dozing off. At no time did he feel angry at his mother for leaving him alone, or for that matter his father. He was happy that they were together.

The question was why did his parents and Amaji leave for Delhi and stay there for so long?

The story goes back to July 1972 when Sapna, Auntie's first child, was born in Srinagar, nine months after her mother's wedding. As was customary those days, women would deliver their babies at their parent's home. Auntie had also returned to Srinagar at the time of her first delivery. However, as her first child was a girl, her in-laws taunted her for delivering her first child at Srinagar because her move had been unlucky for a male-centric family. Having a male child was considered to be a matter of pride in most families; the Bradoo family of Delhi was no different. Thereafter, 15 months later, at the time of her second delivery, her in-laws had forbidden her to travel to Srinagar. Accordingly, her family in Srinagar was expected to move to Delhi and setup a makeshift accommodation nearby to bring her home at the time of the delivery.

Another question arises: How many mothers would leave their young and only child in late autumn/early winter months of Srinagar alone? Not many, of course! So why did Rani have to do that? Because she had no other way, but to follow her in-laws' wishes and whims! On the basis of her past experience, possibly she did not have many options but to accompany her husband and her mother-in-law and provide them her support at Delhi.

In November 1973, the final Year 7 examination began at the school. On several mornings, as breakfast, Billu ate the overnight leftover cold rice with green chillies and salt. During the examination period, he developed chest infection and cough, and perhaps fever. He threw out thick, green coloured, phlegm every time he coughed. His wind pipe felt sour on coughing, with a burning sensation.

Boba arrived from Delhi in early December 1973, just one day before the announcement of his results. On the day of the result, Billu sat in the first row of his class as usual and waited for the Form Teacher to announce the results. Suddenly, Boba appeared outside the classroom door and introduced himself to the teacher. A big smile appeared on his face, as the teacher seemed to explain something to him, which Billu could not hear. Their conversation was not audible from a distance. As the teacher turned back towards the class, Boba raised his index finger and indicated to Billu that he had stood first in the class. Overwhelmed, tears welled up in his eyes. His mind went blank even as he heard his name being announced by the teacher as the first position holder. Despite facing a very tough two-month period before the examination, Billu had proved to himself, and to the world, that his previous success in Year 6 had not been a one-off fluke. He thanked his personal deity for looking after him!

After leaving the classroom, Billu walked with his father across the school ground which had numerous patches of greenish brown grass. It was a sunny morning and the mild sun comforted and soothed him. He tried to soak in as much warmth as he could. During the last month or so, his body had not received hot food or external warmth. From time to time, while walking, he coughed and spewed out thick green clots of phlegm. His physical sick conditions could, however, not take any bit away from his internal joy. Now that he had seen the real light in his life after a long time, all that mattered to him was to keep doing well in his studies; nothing else mattered.

Boba took him to a doctor that afternoon, who prescribed a five-day dose of antibiotics. Two days later, they left for Delhi, first by bus up to Jammu and then by train from there. This was the first time when he had left the valley and it was his first experience aboard a train.

Delhi looked like an entirely different world to his young eyes—warm and nice, with houses that looked like boxes and flat roofed; and smelt different, with phenyl and garlic. The soil did not become muddy after a shower, unlike Srinagar. The whole air was different but nice.

The kids looked different, with straight black oily hair and a darker complexion. They spoke in Hindi and did not wear much woollen clothing unlike Kashmiri kids in Srinagar. However, like Srinagar, they also played street cricket and marbles, both of which he really enjoyed. Soon he made many friends in the neighbourhood. Unlike Srinagar, people ate lots of snack food from street vendors.

A couple of weeks later, Billu watched *Bobby*, a super hit Bollywood movie. This film provided him his with first introduction to the world of romance; he felt like a different person from inside after leaving the cinema hall. The kid in him had perhaps met the man inside.

The family returned to Srinagar in March 1974. Billu resumed his Year 8 class.

In the spring of 1975, the family moved back to their ancestral home in Alikadal. It was a different world. All their neighbours were Muslims; very friendly. Everybody knew the family. He felt at home. Other than school, cricket was the other activity which he enjoyed.

With newly gained confidence and leadership skills, Billu made up a cricket team from a group of same-aged kids in the neighbourhood, about equal in number from both Pandit and Muslim communities. Most of the Pandit kids belonged to the Munshi Mohalla, not far from his home. They played cricket everywhere, in the front courtyard of his house; in the front yard of Munshi Mohalla; in a large public open space between his house and the Munshi Mohalla, where they made the tiled, paved pedestrian path a cricket pitch; the tiled paved narrow street in front of Munshi Mohalla; and at the Idgah grounds, where they played inter-team cricket matches. It was a nice world!

For his Year 9 and Year 10 classes, Boba bought a large number of text books for him from Darya Ganj, Delhi.

Due to his poor rote skills, he never enjoyed History as a course subject; he was poor at remembering the dates. As for Geography, he enjoyed it; due to its more scientific content and the structure.

Unlike most students at that time, he never had a private tutor. It was expected that Tathaji would coach him, being a reputed teacher. But that did not happen. Large groups of students would come home every day for coaching from Tathaji, however, Billu never joined them. On the contrary, Boba pro-actively spent a considerable time in coaching him, though not on a regular basis. Boba's method of coaching was more of a conceptual nature, where he would try to clear his basic concepts of a mathematical or scientific problem. Boba would use very interesting and unique analogies in his coaching method, which perfectly suited Billu. Boba would most often give him spot tests and he was always expected to be ready to take them, with 100% correct answers.

Both Boba and Tathaji taught him that there were no hard and fast methods for solving a problem; one could use any logical method out of a range of the methods available. This lesson from his father and grandfather encouraged him to think deeply as well as laterally and come out with a range of solutions to a problem.

In November 1975, after his annual Year 9 examination, he again found himself at the top of his class. The scenario was no different the following year.

A few days before the start of his Year 10 Board Examination, Billu suddenly became bedridden due to high fever, which lasted for several days and well into the first half of the examination period.

On examination days, Boba carried him to his designated examination centre (SP College, Srinagar), wrapped in a shawl. He would then hand over a bottle of water and a strip of paracetamol tablets to his examination superintendent and then wait outside the examination hall for three hours.

When the results of the Board Matriculation Examinations were announced, in late February 1977, Billu stood first in his school. He scored 629 marks, but fell short of the third position in the Board, by perhaps 50 marks or so, much to his disappointment. At the time of passing his Board Matriculation Examinations, Billu had no clue about his future career as he had never thought about it. One day, Boba advised him that if he did well in his Year 11 examination, he could enter an engineering college.

In March 1977, Billu joined a number of bright new students who had moved from other private schools (Biscoe Tyndale Memorial and Burnhall schools) in his Year 11 class, called Pre-University Course, at DAV Institute. The school year passed very fast. The final Board Examination results were declared in mid to late February 1978. Billu again fell short of the third position by 11 marks. This time he had no big excuse; he was simply beaten by the best in his batch. He was humbled and, luckily, just in time.

In May 1978, Billu sat for the Entrance Examination for REC Srinagar. He passed the examination and was invited to attend an interview on a certain date in June 1978. In the meantime, Boba applied for his admission to several other RECs in India, as admission to REC Srinagar was not assured.

Two day before the interview, on his way home, Billu ate some snacks at a popular *halwai* shop at Lal Chowk. By 4 pm, he had an upset stomach. Due to excessive loss of body water and salts, he started showing symptoms of dehydration and muscle cramps. Those days, as usual, Auntie and her whole family from Delhi were on their annual visit. By around 10 pm, Billu's condition had worsened and the family panicked.

A well-known compounder from a nearby pharmacy injected him with anti-vomiting drug and put him on Intravenous (IV) rehydration treatment. Around 11.30 pm, when Billu had already received three bottles of the rehydration fluid, he vomited again, at which time he heard some family members crying. With hardly any energy left in his slumped body, he slowly opened his eyes to look around. His parents, grandparents, Auntie and Uncle Ashok had all assembled around his bed; everybody looked desperate and helpless. Outside, a heavy downpour continued. The seasoned compounder immediately gave him one more *perinorm* (a branded anti-vomit drug) injection dose and continued the IV rehydration treatment. After that, Billu fell asleep.

As destined, he did not die that night. Due to significant depletion of his energy levels, he remained bedridden for the next 32 hours.

On the morning of the interview day (for admission to REC Srinagar), Boba advised him only one thing, 'Billu, when you enter the interview room, there will be many people sitting around the table and they will ask you many questions. Just listen to one person at a time and try to clearly understand the question before you open your mouth. If you don't follow the question for the first time, politely request the question to be repeated or rephrased. And, yes, one most important thing—the interviewers will possibly not know more than you; so just relax and confidently answer their questions, believing you are their teacher.' With that *mantra*, he left for his interview. As usual, Boba accompanied him to the venue and waited outside the building till he came out. The *mantra* worked.

As the admission list of REC Srinagar was still some time away, Boba bought tickets for both to travel to Kurukshetra, Delhi and Jaipur for exploring the chances of his admission to local colleges in those three places. Amaji was not very happy to see them go. She said, 'Why are you people wasting time and energy? Billu will be selected in Srinagar only. Don't go.'

At REC Kurukshetra, although he was the highest rank holder from the J & K state, the college authorities initially denied him admission because they had *Higher Secondary* qualification as the minimum requirement for admission to the 5-year Bachelor of Engineering degree course, and not the PUC. However, the Higher Secondary system had already been scrapped in J & K a few years ago. On Boba's strong request, they called the competent authority in Srinagar, following which Billu was considered to be eligible for admission.

On the basis of a stressful experience, Boba was not entirely convinced if REC Kurukshetra was the right place for the admission, so they travelled to Delhi the next day and visited the Delhi College of Engineering. The cut off mark here was higher than what Billu had and he was deemed to be ineligible.

A day after their DCE experience, they undertook a 6-hour long train journey to Jaipur, to explore the possibility of Billu's admission at REC Jaipur. It was a wet day but Billu was very impressed to see the red sandstone buildings everywhere and distinct red sand that seemed to cover the ground surface everywhere. The college authorities advised them that the admission list would come out in a day or two. In anticipation of his admission though, they visited an undergraduate student hostel block accompanied by a courteous senior student of the college, who also hosted them later at lunch in the mess. Boba approved of the college and decided to wait. They returned to Auntie's home in Delhi by the evening train.

Overnight, Boba decided to return to Kurukshatra and confirm Billu's admission there; the main reason being it was the nearest interstate college to Srinagar.

Around 10 am, while taking a shower in the bathroom, Billu heard a repeated knock at his bathroom door. Hiding himself behind the door, he opened the latch and he stuck his head out. Auntie stood outside the door with a telegram in her hand. She beamed with joy, with a big broad smile on her face. With a loud happy voice, she congratulated him. Amaji's prediction had been proven right!

Billu was very excited with the news and looked forward to returning to Srinagar. Boba returned from Kurukshetra in the evening; he had already paid the admission fee. However, when he heard about Billu's admission to REC Srinagar, he was very happy. Two days later, they flew to Srinagar by the first flight from Delhi. Rani appeared to be over the moon when she saw him. She kissed Billu on his forehead. Amaji shouted excitedly, 'Didn't I say to you people that Billu will get admission here only?' Tathaji had already left for REC Srinagar campus. It was the cut-off day for necessary paperwork and the payment of admission fee. Tathaji hugged Billu and patted him on his shoulder when he saw him in college. His eyes shone with joy.

In his own words, on that day, Boba had entrusted the responsibility of Billu's safety, security and success to the nearby Hazratbal shrine.

**College Years**

Billu commenced his undergraduate degree course in engineering in 1978. Barring a few very unpleasant events during five years, those five years perhaps comprised the best time of his early life. About a month after his admission, in mid-September 1978, Amaji passed away due to a sudden cardiac arrest while eating dinner. It was the first day of an official 3-day cricket match which Billu was playing at Kashmir University Campus and Billu's team had been fielding on that day. In the evening at home, he asked for early dinner. Amaji started eating her dinner after he had finished eating. Half way through her dinner, she complained of restlessness and soon collapsed in Boba's arms.

She was cremated the next day. This was the first death that Billu had seen in the family.

Tathaji passed away at Jyotipuram near Reasi (Jammu), coincidentally also due to a sudden cardiac arrest while eating lunch in 1983. Those days, Boba was the Engineer in charge for the concrete dam, which was being constructed at the Salal Hydroelectric Project site in Dhyangarh. Reportedly, that afternoon, Boba had a guest from the US over lunch. Tathaji was also seated around the dining table. Half way during the lunch, Boba left his seat to receive a telephone call from the site. When he returned to his seat, he found Tathaji slumped in his seat with his head bent forward. Boba called him by his name but there was no response from the other end.

On the day of the cremation, NHPC engineers from across the country followed his funeral procession. The road between Reasi and Jyotipuram was closed. He was cremated on the banks of River Chandrabagha (aka Chinab). On that day, Billu was in Karnataka on an educational visit to the Krishna Raja Sagara dam site constructed by Sir Visvesvaraya. Tathaji had given him pocket money for the tour.

Billu completed his undergraduate degree in Civil Engineering in exactly five years, despite a number of college closures during that time, most of which were due to local and international political reasons. Several past batches had taken six or more years to graduate. A month after his final examinations, he joined Gammons India Limited. He did not like the bullying behaviour of his boss and two months later joined the J & K state government, as an ad hoc engineer. He soon discovered that he was not thick skinned enough to survive in that environment. In 1984, he responded to a job advertisement for a teaching position at REC Srinagar. Seven teachers were employed, all from his batch. He enjoyed teaching and it did not take him long to discover a teacher in him, like Tathaji.

## A Heartbreak

In the summer of 1980, Billu met a young woman from Delhi named Sanjana. Billu liked her.

Next year in May, she and her mother were in Srinagar again. Billu felt attracted but he did not say anything. Being an only child, he had always longed for a close companion with whom he could share his feelings. A few days later, he wrote a letter to Sanjana and expressed his feelings for her. She immediately reciprocated with a letter expressing similar feelings. That was the beginning of a long series of correspondence between the two. He would show all her letters to Tathaji, who admired her command over the English language.

Boba met Sanjana's father in the city and came to know about the correspondence between the two. He was not happy and told Billu to concentrate on his studies. By the time Billu graduated and began working, the relationship was over for various reasons. Billu then decided to get married to another girl called Rekha.

## 1986

Billu and Rekha met for the first time in an arranged get together on a jetty overlooking Dal Lake in 1986. To test her thinking, he asked her opinion about the future of Kashmiri Pandits in Srinagar in the backdrop of the recent attacks on Pandits living in the Anantnag district of Kashmir. She was right on the money; she said Pandits would have to leave the valley soon and also provided her reasons thereof. This was his partner, Billu thought.

Billu's wedding ceremony was performed with great pomp and show. After the wedding, Billu was scheduled to leave for Roorkee for his post-grad studies. Rekha decided to join him and by August 1986, the young couple moved into their first home in Roorkee.

Billu's weight exploded from 64 kg at the time of his wedding to about 92 kg within six months, courtesy Rekha and the delicious food that she cooked. In June 1987, their son Baba was born in Srinagar. At the end of his studies, the family stayed for a few weeks in Delhi before returning home to Srinagar in 1988.

Marriage, a child, a good job, parents and friends did not, however, give Billu the sense of security ordinary people have under normal circumstances. As violence in Kashmir grew and the general disruption of life in and around Srinagar increased, Billu's sense of insecurity grew. Earlier, if he had felt unsafe for himself, now he was also insecure regarding the wellbeing of his young family. Within months, the situation was so bad that Billu's one thought was to get away from Srinagar as quickly and quietly as possible, this time with his wife and son. The paranoia grew until in December 1989, just a year later, Billu drove himself to craft his and his family's escape out of the valley.

# A Refugee in India—
# Jammu & Delhi

*While a man says not a word*
*His fault and virtue are concealed.*
*Think not that every desert is empty.*
*Possibly it may contain a sleeping tiger.*
—Sa'di (Gulistan)

**January 1990, New Delhi**

After having arrived in Delhi on the evening of 23 December 1989, Billu and his family began their life of migrant Kashmiris. They first took shelter with Delhi-based relatives and then found rented accommodation. Relatives gave them bedding and cooking utensils.

Billu started applying for work with renewed energy and zeal. He had his first job interview in the second week of January 1990, followed by a second interview within about a week. At that stage, his appointment looked imminent. Around the same time, Rekha was successful in securing an academic research position at the prestigious Lady Irwin College. She went to work for about a week and then, unfortunately, had to suddenly stop due to logistical issues at home. As usually happens with women, Rekha was the one who sacrificed her career in the interest of her family, despite being as good and as employable as her husband. The family had not evolved yet to a level where her career would be seen as a priority. Billu began travelling around to look for a job.

Back in Srinagar, Auntie's daughter, Sapna, who lived with Billu's family in Srinagar in 1989, was still waiting to take her Chemistry practical Board examination of Year 12. Due to a bomb blast and some violent demonstrations by agitators, the examination was not conducted as per the original schedule and was postponed indefinitely by the Board.

In the first week of February 1990, Billu, Rekha and Baba visited Jammu to attend a wedding. To a minor extent, it did provide the family with change. For Billu, however, it was a mentally excruciating experience. By late February 1990, Billu had been unable to find a job despite having a number of interviews. His lack of experience in the contracting field proved to be the main impediment. As his cash dwindled fast, he felt desperate. His 2-month lease period for his rental apartment ended in March 1990. Luckily, he had found another rental property in the same lane not far away, which was also relatively cheaper than the first one. For an ordinary fourth storey *barsati* unit (a room on a roof top), the monthly rent was Rupees 1,800, with two months' rent as security deposit. Billu was left with almost nothing in hand. The unit comprised two rooms and a kitchenette, with a detached bathroom and a toilet on the terrace.

For the first time in his life, Billu felt poor and helpless and hoped it was only a nightmare. But the reality about his new-found poverty gradually started sinking in; his world had indeed changed. Small things which he would take for granted in the past in Srinagar had now become a luxury. He developed a deeper empathy for the poor and an understanding of their mindset, now that he was also one of them.

Why was he forced to abandon his home and job in Srinagar? What was his fault other than being a Hindu in Kashmir? Why was God so unfair? Did God really exist? Will the guilty go unpunished? Such questions haunted him several times each day.

Slowly he began to reconcile with his new environment and home; he started looking at the positives to keep himself afloat.

**Even Boba Leaves Srinagar**

On a Friday, 19 January 1990, Boba was on a work tour of various fish farms at Kokernag, in South Kashmir. Those days, he was the Executive Engineer with the Fisheries Department, on deputation from the Roads & Building (R & B) Department. His work required him to travel far and wide as his jurisdiction was the entire state of Jammu & Kashmir. At the Kokernag trout farm, the department had set up a new fully mechanised feed mill, funded and supplied by the European Economic Community.

Twice during the day, while Boba was away from the house, a Muslim colleague of his called the house number from Delhi and, in Boba's absence, spoke to Rani. He requested that they (Boba and Rani) should fly to Delhi for a month or so for a change. This person's younger brother also called once and conveyed the same message on behalf of his brother.

Boba returned home from work around 9 pm. He had bought fresh lamb's meat from Kokernag for the weekend. Being Friday, Rani put the meat in the fridge as she was on fast on that day. She apprised him about the phone calls and the messages from Mr Rasheed and his younger brother. As it was too late in the day to call Rasheed or his brother, and as he was very tired after a long work day, Boba decided to call Rasheed in the morning. They ate their dinner and then watched a late night movie on the television. Those days, *Doordarshan,* India's first government run television channel, would telecast late night movies on Fridays.

Next morning, the phone rang again, around 7 am. It was Rasheed's younger brother on the line. He reiterated his brother's message and requested Boba once again to move to Delhi for a few days, if not for anything else, just for a change of weather.

Boba had known Rasheed and his family very well for more than a decade. The repeated phone calls from Rasheed and his younger brother made Boba apprehensive about the reasons why he was being requested to leave the valley. The said reason, just for a change, did not seem plausible. A thought flashed through his mind; Boba decided to walk across the street and see his immediate neighbour (a Muslim doctor, known as Doctor Sahib) to know what was going on. When they met, Doctor Sahib asked him, 'Koul Sahib, are you sure that you don't know that Kashmir did not sleep last night? Did you not hear anything from the loud speaker of our local masjid?' Thereafter, Doctor Sahib told Boba about the volatile situation in the valley.

Boba was shaken from the inside and expressed his complete ignorance, telling Doctor Sahib about his own movements during the previous day. Doctor Sahib told him, 'Koul Sahib, please come with me; let us walk together up to Rawalpora Chowk and assess the current situation.' Rawalpora Chowk is at a distance of about 1 km from the Koul house. On the way, Boba noticed the ominous presence of an unusually large number of groups of men, huddled close together in each group. As they passed these groups, Boba noticed that the men would turn around and look conspicuously at them. The group sizes varied from two to more than ten persons. Boba suddenly became tense and his heart beat faster. Disquiet on the street meant something untoward and unprecedented was imminent.

Rani and Boba had brought up Sapna like their own daughter. In their eyes, she had somewhat filled the gap as the daughter of the family, given that Rani had not been able to bear any other child after Billu. Many of their friends, and Billu's relatives from his in-laws side, were made to believe that Sapna was their daughter. In a volatile situation like this, when danger appeared to be looming large all around, Sapna's physical protection took the utmost priority for Boba. After all, she was a member of the Bradoo family and not his daughter; he decided that he could not take any chance whatsoever in regard to her safety. Had Sapna not been living with them at that time, Boba would have waited for some more time for the clouds to disperse and for a clearer picture to emerge. With these thoughts flashing through his agitated mind, Boba did not take much time to decide what he must do to ensure that Sapna was quickly returned safely to her parents in Delhi.

After completing their reconnaissance walk, on returning home, Boba asked Doctor Sahib, 'Doctor Sahib, we have the flight tickets for Delhi later this morning. Will you be kind enough to drop us at the airport?' As usual, Doctor Sahib was ready to assist without any hesitation.

On entering his house, Boba firmly closed the door behind him and shouted, with urgency in his voice, 'Rani, please stop cooking. Pack a couple of bags at once, only one each for you and me. Ask Sapna to pack all her bags. We must leave for the airport in the next half an hour. Doctor Sahib has agreed to drop us there. Carry all your valuables with you; don't leave anything in the home.'

Rani looked perplexed and asked in disbelief, 'But why? What has suddenly happened? Why are you panicking? We have just started our day and not even eaten our breakfast yet.

I am also cooking the lamb that you bought yesterday from Kokernag.'

Boba replied with desperation in his voice, 'Rani, please don't waste any time in asking me any further questions; just do what I am begging you to do. Leave everything as it is. Give the lamb to the tenants. Inform them that we need to fly to Delhi urgently and request them to look after the house in our absence. I'll explain everything to you later on the plane. Also, before leaving home, please remove the *bindi* from your forehead (the red dot Hindu women wear on the forehead) and cover your head to look like a Muslim woman. Pretend to be sick and keep coughing as we drive to the airport. Ask Sapna also to cover her head.'

As Rani got busy in packing, Boba called the airport and asked if it was functioning that morning. He was advised that the airport was functioning as normal and the flights were arriving from Delhi as scheduled. Boba would be able to leave only if he could reach the airport on time, as curfew had been imposed by the government in several parts of the city.

Within the next 45 minutes or so, Boba, Rani and Sapna were seated in Doctor Sahib's Maruti car, which had a very limited baggage space. Doctor Sahib drove the car. Rani was seated on the back seat of the car, with Sapna by her side. The airport was about 6 km from their home. On their way to the airport, they were greeted by numerous processions, with people shouting anti-India and pro-freedom slogans. The car had to be stopped at a number of places due to road blockades by people. On such occasions, they would roll down the window and request the crowd to let them drive through to the airport, as the lady (pointing towards Rani) was very sick and had to be urgently flown out for medical treatment. She faked a deep and persistent cough to facilitate the passage. Rani, with her head fully covered and without any *bindi* on her forehead, appeared to be like a typical Kashmiri Muslim woman. On one occasion, someone from the crowd shouted, 'Tell these bastards in Delhi that they must immediately leave Kashmir.'

On reaching the airport, when the security personnel asked for the tickets, Boba found himself in an extremely embarrassing situation; he had no tickets. He looked at Doctor Sahib with an extremely apologetic face but Doctor Sahib said nothing. He understood. Boba alighted from the car and pointed towards Rani and said that she was very sick and had to be flown to Delhi for urgent medical attention. Like before, Rani faked a persistent and deep cough. Boba showed them his government identity card. The security personnel advised him that the plane waiting on the terminal was bound for Jammu, and not Delhi.

Boba quickly pleaded, 'That is fine, she needs to be flown to any warmer place. It does not matter if it is Jammu or Delhi, either will do.' On hearing this, the security personnel said, 'Okay, we can let her go, but not you.' With desperation, Boba pleaded again, 'But Sir, she is unable to travel alone in her current sick condition; she will need assistance, so I must accompany her. And, yes, we can't leave our daughter behind. Please let both of us accompany her.' The drama worked. He got a nod from the security personnel to move ahead to the terminal building.

After all disembarked from the car on reaching the terminal building, Boba thanked Doctor Sahib for his kind gesture and deeply apologised to him for lying about the tickets. As a true gentleman, Doctor Sahib did not say anything. After they exchanged their farewell hug, Boba walked towards the airport terminal building, with embarrassment still lurking in his mind. He wondered what Doctor Sahib would think about him.

On reaching Jammu, they headed straight for Jammu Railway Station and bought tickets on an overnight train to Delhi.

The next day was Sunday, 21 January 1990. Sapna was safely handed over to her family. Boba's responsibility regarding his sister's daughter had been taken care of. He did not want to stay back in Delhi. Without discussing with anyone, Boba went to the nearest airline booking office at Safdarjung Airport, and bought return flight tickets for himself and Rani for 29 January 1990. He agreed to spend 26 January, the Republic Day of India in Delhi. Billu was clearly not very pleased with his decision and strongly voiced his dissent. As usual, Boba did not listen.

During that week, however, disturbing news about hordes of people leaving Kashmir arrived on a daily basis. By the evening of 26 January, Boba's decision to fly back to Srinagar on the coming Monday morning appeared to be just madness. Considering that hordes of people were coming out daily, his decision to return to Srinagar was against common sense, ridiculous and illogical, Billu thought. It alarmed everyone. After repeated persuasion, Boba was forced to visit the airline office on Saturday evening to cancel his tickets. However, he did not give up; he rebooked his return tickets for 12 February 1990.

During that fortnight, Boba met his colleague, Rasheed, who again tried to dissuade him from returning to Srinagar. By now, the disturbing news of the mass exodus of the Pandit families from Kashmir had become a daily news item. Once again, albeit with some reluctance, Boba cancelled his flight just a day before the scheduled departure. Boba and Rani decided to continue to stay at Delhi till some further direction arrived from his boss.

However, no one could hold him for long in Delhi and soon he was back in Kashmir. Within a short time he was back in his job, this time working out of Jammu.

In Jammu, since their arrival from Delhi in May, Boba and Rani initially lived for a month at Hotel Airlines, near Jewel

Chowk. They ate at the local *dhabas*. Many of their relatives had taken up temporary rental accommodations in various localities across Jammu. By now, they had finally realised that their return to Srinagar was virtually impossible. They felt desperate and made a plan to salvage some of their important belongs from their 3-storey house in Srinagar.

One day, around mid-May, without even discussing the matter first with Billu and Rekha, Rani flew from Jammu to Srinagar by an afternoon flight. She was received at the airport by Boba's colleague, Sardar J S Bali, and his mother. In the meantime, Boba had despatched two empty taxis to Srinagar. The plan was that the taxis would reach their Rawalpora house that evening where Rani would receive them. The plan worked well. Rani loaded the two taxis with only the essential items, leaving everything else behind. The Bali family assisted her. The two loaded taxis were despatched back to Jammu that very evening and Rani stayed overnight with the Bali family. Next morning, she flew back to Jammu as scheduled. On reaching Jammu, she noticed that a Persian silk carpet was missing.

When the news of Rani's adventurous trip to Srinagar was broken to Billu, he cried bitterly and became very angry with his parents. Over the phone, he lashed out at his father, 'Why did you send my mother alone to Srinagar? What if something untoward would have happened to her? Her life is much more precious than all those things that she has salvaged. You have been so irresponsible. Why didn't you first discuss your plans with me?' Boba, of course, had nothing to say.

Soon, in Delhi, however, Billu's eyes yearned to see green grass. Kashmir seemed to be a distant dream of the past. All Kashmiri Pandits living outside Kashmir are migrants, whether new or old migrants. It is quite sad that, while most old Kashmiri Pandit migrants, who had settled in Delhi before 1990 and many non-Kashmiri Indians were quite helpful and sympathetic to the new Kashmiri Pandit migrants of 1990, there was a section of the old Kashmiri Pandit migrant community who displayed a total lack of empathy (rather showed disdain) towards their fellow community members who had been uprooted from Kashmir in 1990.

One Sunday morning of July 1990, when Billu and Rekha were visiting Auntie, she had a visitor, a Kashmiri Pandit lady in her early fifties. This lady had been living in Delhi for more than three decades. During their conversation over morning tea, the lady said she was looking for a suitable match for her daughter and asked Auntie if she knew about any. Incidentally, Auntie had recently come to know about such a possible match. She said, 'I know about a handsome boy, from a good family, who has recently arrived from Jammu and joined a multinational engineering company in Delhi at a good position. The parents are well educated and have recently migrated from Srinagar to Jammu.' When the lady heard this, she frowned and replied sarcastically, '*Main in bukhe-nango ko apne beti nahi doongee* (I am not giving my daughter to these beggars).' Auntie was shocked to hear this, as were the other people present on the occasion.

Around this time, some matrimonial advertisements in *Koshur Samachar* clearly notified, 'Migrants need not to apply.' Some Pandits had obviously forgotten that all Kashmiri Pandits living outside Kashmir were migrants, whether old or new.

It was a hazy time for the family. Unlike the locals, they had no real experience with the living conditions outside Kashmir, especially the sicknesses and the diseases which are common during the monsoon season.

**November 1990**
Rekha was expecting her second baby and Billu and his wife decided to join his parents in Jammu for the delivery. They travelled by train from Delhi and by the time they arrived at

their first home in Jammu, it was already dark on that November day of 1990. Following a suggestion from his boss, a month after returning from Delhi, Boba had moved into the second storey of a guesthouse at the fish farm of the Fisheries Department, located on the northern bank of River Tawi. It was only in the morning, when Billu peeped out of his bedroom window that he realised how beautiful the surroundings were.

The farm was well laid out and pristine. It featured a number of fish ponds, lush green lawns, numerous flower beds, an overhead large water tank and an office building. To Billu's tired eyes, the farm appeared to be a paradise. His wish for green grass was answered! The lush green lawns and the beautiful flowers reminded him of his lost home in Srinagar. The air appeared fresh and clean, with absolutely no comparison to the Delhi air. The vehicular noise was nowhere to be heard, thankfully. Just up to a day ago, such a pictorial setting had been a distant dream. He thought he was very lucky to be there after so many months of living in relatively harsh conditions and in a place where only grey concrete structures were visible. The water supply from the overhead tank provided cold water 24 hours a day. It was fed by a purpose-built pump house located within the farm. The power supply, provided by an emergency power supply line, was relatively uninterrupted as it had to meet the requirements of the aquarium located on the ground floor of the guesthouse, and the fish ponds. This farm was one of several fish farms in the state that had been developed by the Fisheries Department in the past decade or so under the engineering leadership of Boba. During the development of this farm, he would have never imagined that one day it would become his first home in Jammu.

Billu had heard that the camp office of the REC Srinagar had just started its operations in Jammu, within the premises of a polytechnic campus, to help the displaced students. When Billu went there, he received warm smiles and hugs by his colleagues and the students who knew him from Srinagar. Professor Parbin Singh was the coordinator of the Camp Classes. In November 1990, the students of Second Year (3$^{rd}$ Semester), Third Year (5$^{th}$ Semester) and Fourth Year (7$^{th}$ Semester) were studying at REC Camp Classes, Jammu.

A significant number of non-Muslim students and staff had left the (main) Srinagar campus of the REC for fear of their lives. The students belonging to the other states of India had been adjusted by their local RECs. Many non-Muslim students from Jammu & Kashmir had also been absorbed by those colleges; however, a considerable number of students had returned to Jammu, as they did not adjust in those colleges for a range of reasons. On their return to Jammu, they demanded that Camp Classes be operated in Jammu. To press their demands, the protesting students had also resorted to a hunger strike which lasted for several weeks. Finally, the then state government and the REC administration had given in to their demands and allowed the start of REC Srinagar Camp Classes at Jammu. In the autumn session of 1990, the students of three batches (3$^{rd}$, 5$^{th}$ and 7$^{th}$ semester), in all streams of Engineering (Civil, Electrical, Electronics, Mechanical and Chemical), had to be looked after. It was not a very easy task, considering that only skeleton teaching staff was available in each stream of engineering, which had to cover all the subjects. In addition, laboratory facilities had to be borrowed from the colleges outside Jammu. Having a blackboard and a classroom was a luxury.

Billu quickly learnt that the college administration was struggling to provide teaching facilities to Civil Engineering students, as only four staff members were available to share a full-fledged teaching load of the three batches. No one was available to teach the units related to Soils & Foundations Engineering, as well as Highway and Transportation engineering. These units fell under Billu's area of specialisation; it was a relief for everyone to see him return. For Billu, the opportunity was God-sent. He could do his bit towards helping the students, who faced grave uncertainty and whose future was at stake.

The first Camp Classes in Jammu (at the Polytechnic) comprised a two-storey building, located in a corner of the campus, with about eight rooms. In addition, two class rooms from the Polytechnic facility were available to the REC classes from time to time. A roof-top concrete water tank and the rusted side of an old abandoned bus were also used by teachers as make-shift blackboards. It was a common scenario to see a teacher sitting on grass in the middle of the ground and the students (15 or more) squatting around him/her.

On his first day at the Camp Classes, Billu became very emotional. He actually cried, thinking of the conditions under which REC now had to run. No one deserved to be in that situation; these students were engineering students after all, no joke! He felt very concerned for their future. He had to start immediately, as the final semester examinations were due in about a month's time; there was no time left. He had a job offer in Delhi when he had brought Rekha to Jammu. He called off the offer.

Striving earnestly, Billu was able to cover a number of subjects to a reasonable extent within whatever time was left before the onset of semester examination. All his other colleagues, both academic and administrative, put their hearts and souls into their work, despite their personal hardships, as most of them were themselves migrants (a term coined by the government for the *internally displaced people* from Kashmir). For most of the teachers and administration staff, the world seemed to be burning but they put their sufferings aside and steadfastly stuck to their respective duties. The question papers arrived from the main campus in Srinagar and were sent back to Srinagar for marking. The examination was not only for testing the students; in practical context it was also tested how well the teachers had done their work. To everyone's delight and satisfaction, most students passed with good grades. That winter, the students completed their laboratory work at various technical institutions in north India under the supervision of their home staff.

Deeksha was born on Christmas Day, 1990.

While Rekha and Deeksha were still at the nursing home, Professor P N Kachroo arrived from Srinagar. He handed over a cash cheque of a decent amount of money to Billu in lieu of his input to the Geotechnical Consultancy Team on a number of projects before his sudden departure from Srinagar. That cheque was timely. Billu had forgotten all about his consultancy work. Thanks to Professor Kachroo, its arrival was a welcome surprise. The arrival of the cheque from Srinagar signalled that his daughter had brought her own share of luck and fortune for her parents. Philosophically, it was apparent that he, as a parent, was only a custodian of her fortune that she had been brought with her. The Koul family started living a relatively better life from then on.

**Boba Maama leaves Srinagar**

Rani loved her only brother Boba Maama, much more than anyone else in the world.

It had been about a year since most of the Pandits had left the valley but he had chosen not to leave and was still residing in his house at Bagat Barzulla. Rani remained constantly worried about his welfare and concerned for his safety. She would call her brother and sister-in-law on a daily basis and they would assure her that they were absolutely safe and that there was nothing to be worried about. Despite their assurances, Rani would remain restless and tense. Out of sheer helplessness and desperation, caused by her brother's seemingly careless disposition, her love for him had now begun to transform into anger. Thankfully, their two daughters, Meenu and Neelu, had already left Kashmir in January 1990, courtesy Kak uncle and Kak auntie, who had strongly persuaded their parents to allow them to accompany the Kak family to Ghaziabad in UP.

Towards the end of January 1991, about a year after the mass exodus of Pandits, Boba Maama and Maamiji finally left Kashmir and arrived at the fish farm. It was such a great relief for Rani and all her family members. It had been more than a year since they had met. Rani was over the moon when she saw him. Her emotional outburst followed a roller coaster; initially she cried and wept with joy, but then shouted angrily at him. Her hugs and kisses alternated with serious angry outbursts, reprimanding him from time to time. This went on for a few days till the dust settled.

Reportedly, in the last quarter of 1990, Boba Maama, who was a popular dentist, had received several death threats from a number of unknown people, who had asked him to leave Kashmir. Before leaving, however, he had consulted two of his Muslim neighbours who were also his good friends. Unfortunately, both neighbours had not been very convincing in assuring him about his safety. One could not blame them. It was a very dark time in the history of Kashmir; no one felt absolutely safe and no one could provide any such guarantee for anyone else's safety. The security personnel were themselves the targets. Collateral casualties were rampant. God seemed to be sleeping!

The Koul home at the fish farm remained a very busy place for many months of 1991. Many relatives and friends visited them.

In January 1991, the same Muslim couple from Rawalpora, Doctor Sahib and his wife, visited the Koul family at their fish farm residence. They lived across the street in front of the Koul house at Rawalpora. Both families had moved into the area around the same time in 1982.

The gentleman was a government medical doctor and the lady was a school headmistress. In Srinagar, the relationship between the two families had been very cordial, like good neighbours. Doctor Sahib was a thorough gentleman. He used to be frequently consulted by the Koul family, even at odd hours of the day or night. He was the one who had helped Boba and Rani leave Srinagar.

After exchanging customary greetings, followed by warm hugs and kisses, the guests were served afternoon tea with a variety of snacks. During the course of the conversation, the lady suddenly said, 'You Pandits meticulously follow astrology and do everything as per the right *saath* (good omen). The construction of the Pandit houses also always commences on the day of a good *saath*; it is sad that you had to leave those houses.' This careless statement visibly stunned everyone, including Doctor Sahib. Although this comment had caused a deep hurt, Rani maintained her composure as a good host, and gently replied, 'Yes, my sister, it is really unfortunate that we had to leave our home and hearth in Kashmir. But, if we think about it, is it not because of our belief in the astrology and our religious practices that we could safely move out of the valley, unlike our Muslim brothers who are unfortunately caught between the militants and the security forces?' The blank expression on the lady's face revealed her discomfort; she had not expected such a strong but soft response from Rani. From his body language and the tone of conversation, it seemed Doctor Sahib had empathy for the Kouls and genuinely felt sorry and concerned at the plight of the Pandits.

Towards the end, the lady made another passing remark, 'Now that you people have left Kashmir, you have still given very Kashmiri names to your children (*Kongposh and Shang-e-asham*)'. No one from the Koul family responded. The lady had subsequently met Behanji in Srinagar. On seeing Behanji crying bitterly about her displaced relatives, she had tried to console her with, 'Please don't cry. They are residing in Shalimar Bagh (ie. the largest Mughal garden in Srinagar, laid by the bank of Dal Lake)'.

In the spring of 1991, the REC Camp Classes were moved to a couple of newly-constructed residential buildings in an upcoming suburb named Channi Himmat. On the lines of the main campus in Srinagar, the Camp Classes were also provided with two new 18-seater buses for transporting the staff between the main residential areas in the city and the new campus. The new facilities made life so much easier for the staff. But the same could not be said about the students; they had to rely on the public transport, which was not very efficient in that area at that time.

During the months of April to July, the Channi Himmat area, being very open, arid and relatively low lying, was hotter than the older, higher parts of Jammu city. The bright and scorching sun was unbearable. One felt like one was being roasted alive while moving outdoors during the day. A day did not pass when most people did not suffer from nostalgia about their homeland. The harsh climatic conditions had created a sickening feeling in the émigré people, Mother Kashmir had abandoned them.

In July 1991, the semester examinations at the REC were held as per the schedule for the students of $4^{th}$, $6^{th}$ and $8^{th}$ semesters. With this, the Camp Classes delivered their first batch of graduate students. It was an outstanding achievement for one and all involved with the Camp Classes. Of course, it was a great relief for the new graduates!

During the month of July 1991, when REC Camp Classes closed for the summer break, the Koul family escaped to the nearby hill stations of Patnitop and Kud, for about a couple of weeks, in order to find some quick relief from the hot and humid climate of Jammu. They were accompanied by Auntie and her family from Delhi.

In those early days, Pandits had very poor skills in tackling unfamiliar and harsh weather conditions. Diseases and sicknesses amongst the Pandits, some even life-threatening, became a common affair. These included heat strokes due to the sun; water-borne diseases, such as diarrhoea, dysentery, typhoid; malaria and dengue. Every now and then, the émigré community would receive the sad news of someone's untimely death, many such deaths were from snake bite. This made Billu shudder with fear. Such causalities soon became a common affair amongst the migrants. Some poor victims of snake bites had reportedly not been able to seek help in time and some victims had not been able to differentiate a mosquito bite from a snake bite! Most of such casualties occurred during the dark hours of the night, with the victim either sleeping or pissing near a bush. New place, new adversary, and no survival skills. God was surely sleeping!

Billu had started suffering from a new kind of paranoia in Jammu—about mosquito and snake bites. He would feel stressed if he was bitten by a mosquito for fear of potentially contracting malaria or the dreaded dengue fever. However, in instances where he was not very sure about the mosquito bite, he would get quite stressed and would be afraid that it could be a snake bite. During the next few hours, he would closely monitor himself. With time, of course, he learnt to differentiate between the two types of bites and managed himself reasonably well.

In November 1991, after a great deal of persuasion by his colleagues at the Camp Classes, in particular a friend named Kanwal Kumar Koul, Billu was initiated into Transcendental Meditation (TM) by Bhaisahib (Bansi Lal Hakhu).

After completing his first session of meditation in front of Bhaisahib, Billu felt as if he had wasted all the previous years of this life. He felt like a new person, much lighter in his head, rejuvenated and stable. As it turned out, several of his colleagues at the REC had also been initiated in TM by Bhaisahib, they were his fellow meditators, which he did not know before his initiation. Retrospectively, he learnt why his colleagues did not discuss the usual day-to-day mundane affairs of a Kashmiri in Bhaisahib's company and why they interpreted and addressed issues differently. Before his initiation, he had simply not been able to assess the gravitas of their thinking and conversations.

The REC semester examinations took place at the Camp Classes in December 1991. By March 1992, the REC Camp Classes moved to the Old Jammu University campus at Canal Road. Amazingly, Billu's new work location was now not more than a five-minute walk from his fish farm home. It made life so much easier for him. Rekha was initiated in TM during Guru Days in January 1992. A few months later, Boba was also initiated in TM. Rani took a year more after Boba to get initiated.

The Year 1992 was relatively better than the previous year. People had by now started adapting to their new living conditions in Jammu. Many of Billu's relatives had moved to better rental accommodations across Jammu. Wedding ceremonies were performed with greater pomp and show; it appeared that people were trying to overcompensate for the loss of their home in Kashmir. Billu wondered why people were spending exorbitant amount of their hard earned money on relatively lavish weddings. Shouldn't they be exercising a degree of austerity in their non-essential expenditures, considering that they were displaced from their home? If both the groom's side and the brides' side were Kashmiri migrants, they could amply understand each other's position (seemingly precarious those days) well. So, why could they not sit with each other and decide to perform relatively simpler and joint wedding functions to save unnecessary expenses? Interestingly, many Kashmiris believe themselves to be of Jewish origins. 'Would the Jews also waste their savings and perform wedding ceremonies like Kashmiri migrants?', Billu wondered.

In July 1992, REC Camp Classes delivered their second batch of graduates. These students were in their third year at the time of migration.

Somewhere around late August 1992, the family escaped for two weeks to Dharamsala and explored McLeod Gunj, where the Dalai Lama lived. It resembled the road between Tangmarg and Gulmarg in Kashmir. The group enjoyed a few picnics on those grassed slopes and felt nostalgic about Gulmarg. On alternate days, they would drive down about 10 Km to a nearby beautiful town called Yol, with picturesque views. Yol looked like the Ganderbal area in Kashmir, particularly similar to Wusan, Prang and Hari Ganiwan, as well as Jajjar Kotli near Jammu. After Kashmir, this was the first time they had enjoyed themselves in a glacier-fed, cold water stream, flowing fast through boulders. From time to time, everyone's eyes would well up in memory of their previous life in Kashmir. Children had lots of fun playing in the stream; it was their first experience playing in fast flowing cold water. After a week here they travelled to Dalhousie. The picturesque Dalhousie reminded them of Batote. Khajjiar Lake, about 15 km from Dalhousie, again reminded them strongly of Gulmarg and Yusmarg. One day, while returning from Khajjiar, the family met a Bollywood film shooting crew at Lakkar Mandi, situated about mid-way between Dalhousie and Khajjiar. They were delighted to meet and interact with the actors Sayeed Jaffery and Rajindar Nath; Arman Kohli was the lead actor with a newcomer actresses named Koyal. Next day, the group returned to Lakkar Mandi and enjoyed the shooting. The film crew members and actors were delighted to have Kashmiri *Kahwa* and *Sheer Chai*. As always, good times don't last long. No one looked excited during the return journey to Jammu.

In the autumn of 1993, the REC Camp Classes were allocated the whole of Old Jammu University Campus. Extensive repairs were carried out to the old campus with the assistance and supervision of the Civil Engineering staff of REC Camp Classes. The campus infrastructure was fast upgraded. The skeleton staff of the REC Camp Classes was entrusted with the development of nuts and bolts for the Government College of Engineering, Jammu. Billu and his colleagues found themselves busy in drafting syllabi for various streams of engineering and procurement of laboratory testing equipment for the new institution. They also had the responsibility to oversee and approve civil engineering works being undertaken by civil contractors within the campus.

By the end of December 1993, the Koul family moved to a newly constructed officer's residential quarter within the fish farm, which had much more space than the earlier second-storey guesthouse. It had the ambience of a proper residential house. Around March 1993, Billu applied for a position of Scientist Level 'C' at the prestigious CSIR-Central Road Research Institute CRRI, Mathura Road, New Delhi. To his disbelief, he received a registered envelope from CSIR-CRRI about two weeks after the interview, informing him that he had been successful in winning a position. He was over the moon. In his excitement, he showed the appointment letter to his parents. Boba was also very happy and delighted on receiving the good news but Rani did not look happy. Billu was expected to join within a period of three months. For no particular reason, Billu left the letter with Boba. A senior colleague at REC advised that, instead of resigning from REC, he should request REC to second him to CSIR-CRRI, just in case he decided to return if he did not fit-in at his new work place. Despite trying hard, REC refused to second him.

Towards the end of June 1993, Billu and family took a holiday in Dehradun. They also met Bhisahib's American disciple, Mona Schwartz. In 1975, Mona was diagnosed by the doctors in the US as suffering from a form of blood cancer. She was given six months to survive at the most. Completely rejecting their prognosis, her will power to survive took her to Japan where she started herbal treatment. After that, she travelled to India in search of *jadi-bhuti* (herbal medicine) and finally landed in Srinagar, where she visited REC Srinagar to test some herbs. At REC, she met two lecturers in the Chemical Engineering department, Dr Wanchoo and Dr Razdan. She asked them the reasons behind their radiant faces. They said they meditated regularly. On hearing that, she requested them to teach her the technique of meditation at that very instance.

They told her they were not the qualified teachers of meditation and advised her to learn meditation from their teacher, B L Hakhu (Bhaisahib), who was their colleague. She did not feel very well and wanted a quick fix. Hurriedly, after noting down Bhaisahib's address, she rushed to meet him at his home at Badiyaar. However, on reaching Badiyaar, she met Bhaisahib's namesake who also lived nearby. On knowing the reasons why she wanted to see Hakhu, the gentleman accompanied her to Bhaisahib's home. As soon as she reached there, she collapsed and fainted. She was running a very high temperature. For the next three days, she stayed at Bhaisahib's home till she recovered from fever. Mummyji fed her plenty of fresh orange juice to cool her down. On the third day, Bhaisahib initiated her into TM. Mona returned to her houseboat and later moved to a newly-constructed ashram at Dara, near Harwan, which Bhaisahib had built.

She did not leave Kashmir until one day in Jan 1990 when four English speaking, gun-toting militants barged into the ashram. In her own words, on sensing their intentions to kill her, out of desperation, she picked up a *trishul* (a trident) and started dancing violently like Shiva's *tandav* (dance). Incidentally, at that very moment, the low clouds in the sky rumbled. The militants panicked and their commander asked one of his mates, '*Ye kyo chhe karaan* (what is she doing?)' On seeing panic on their faces, she danced with greater energy like a mad woman. They then fled due to fear.

Within the next ten minutes, she packed a bag and ran towards the main road, where she caught an auto-rickshaw and reached Srinagar. Next day she flew to Delhi where she lived for a couple of months. After March 1990, the unfriendly weather in Delhi was too hot for her to handle, considering her health conditions. In search of a cooler climate, she landed at Rajpur, where she stayed for a number of years. In July 1993, when Billu first meet Mona at Rajpur, she had not fully recovered from cancer, but she had learnt how to manage and keep it under control. She meditated frequently. Her food did not include any dairy product. Her entire family in the US had also stopped the consumption of all dairy products. She mainly consumed brown rice and vegetables.

After meeting Mona, Billu and his party took a train from Dehradun for Jammu. During the night, the train suddenly stopped at Mukarian, in Punjab, as the track ahead was flooded due to an incessant monsoon rainfall. By morning, the flood water had risen to the knee deep level around the train. Several other trains had also stopped on the adjacent tracks. On seemingly war footing, the people of Mukarian tirelessly served all train passengers during that night, and the following day, with uninterrupted delivery of food packets; milk for children; paracetamol for the sick and feverish; and candles and match boxes. It was amazing to see such great human spirit in action in the lovely people of Mukarian. Around 4 pm the next day, the family decided to leave the train and waddled through knee deep water to the nearest road.

Luckily, a truck driver agreed to transport them up to Pathankot on an advance payment of Rupees 500 per person. From there, they took a local bus to Jammu. Reportedly, hundreds of passengers, who had not left Mukarian that afternoon, were held up there for several more days, as a number of railway and road bridges were inundated.

By the end of July 1993, Billu had not been able to resign from the REC, which was necessary to obtain the NOC (no objection certificate). For seeking extension to his joining date at CSIR-CRRI, Billu and his young family visited Delhi in early August 1993. They stayed at the flat they continued to maintain in Delhi. In July 1993, the third and the last batch of the original migrant students completed their undergraduate studies at the REC Camp Classes. In the meantime, two new batches had been admitted by the government during the last couple of years.

Billu kept on asking his father to return his Letter of Appointment from CRRI, but the latter dilly dallied. The extension period expired after a couple of months and, with that, the offer letter lost its validity. He deeply regretted such a missed opportunity. This was the beginning of serious inter-family differences. Rani, his mother, had not been in favour of her grand children moving away from her and had tried to sabotage the move in every possible way that she could.

In the winter of 1993-1994, Bhaisahib's younger son, Anil Hakhu's wedding ceremony was performed at the fish farm. All associated functions, such as *Devgon, Mehandiraat* and the wedding reception were also performed there. The marriage ceremony was characterised by a couple of salient features.

All ceremonies were performed in the traditional Kashmiri Pandit style, in accordance with Bhaisahib's directions. No modern frills and extravaganzas were visible and simplicity was the theme. Meals were served in the lawns of the farm under a shamiana (a canopy). The guests were served individually as per Kashmir traditions. Buffet system was not used.

During the marriage function, Billu had an invaluable interaction with Bhasahib. Those days, the Koul house would be thronged by many Hindi speaking people. Those included the resident fish farm helpers, gardeners, workers of the Fisheries Department, the neighbours, friends and many relatives whose children spoke in Hindi. The overall environment at Jammu had encouraged Billu's children also to speak in Hindi. In contrast, during his first two years at Srinagar, most people in Srinagar spoke to Baba either in English or in Kashmiri.

By the middle of 1994, Boba was very busy. At short notices, he would travel far and wide, and visit fish farms across the entire state of Jammu & Kashmir. In the summer of 1994, as usual, the family planned their annual retreat to Dalhousie. However, one day before they were scheduled to depart, Boba announced that he could not accompany them because of some official work. He told the others to go ahead with their holiday. Billu refused and in frustration, told his father, 'You don't have the time to spend with your family. On the contrary, you have also tied me down. I feel suffocated. Just like a small tree can't grow under the shadow of a large tree, I can't grow and prosper while I am living here in the comfort of this house. I need my own share of the sun, rain, hail storm and wind to grow, which can't happen while I am living here under your patronage. So, I must leave this home and move far away, where you will need a visa to visit us. In India, you people will follow me everywhere.' Boba reluctantly changed his official work itinerary. The family departed for Dalhousie two days later, where they stayed for about a week.

The inter-family disputes eventually took their toll. The Koul home used to be full of guests, some living for a week and some for up to a couple of months or more at a time. One day, Billu's friend, Rajinder, who was a frequent visitor to the house, commented, 'Like Srinagar, here in Jammu also, your house is like a *Dharmshala* (free guesthouse for the needy)'.

The issue was not that the house had constant resident guests; the issue was that most of these guests showed unbridled tendency to exercise their unlawful/unethical right to interfere in the matters of the household that solely pertained to the members of the Koul family. Most guest residents never realised that it was none of their business to meddle in the affairs of the host family. A number of mischievous individuals, with seemingly a free rein, actively tried to use dirty and divisive politics to exploit the interfamily relational strain to their personal advantage. Billu could see their intents clearly but his parents did not; they just enjoyed the company of the (opportunist) guests and the importance that they were receiving from them. Such individuals tactfully flattered and appeased Boba and Rani and, in return, enjoyed a long rope to manoeuvre around the personal affairs of the father and son, mother and daughter-in-law.

One day, in early October 1994, in the presence of an older couple, who had been camping in the Koul house for more than two months at that time, a serious argument broke out between Billu and Boba, following which Billu felt too humiliated to continue staying with his parents and decided to leave immediately. He declared, 'As a small tree can't grow under the shade of a large tree, I can't grow here…I must find my own space.'

Despite Rekha's initial resistance, the family left and moved temporarily in with his in-laws, who lived nearby at Talab Tillo. Boba immediately called his sisters for help; Auntie flew from Delhi and Behanji from Srinagar. Both aunts visited Billu and tried hard to motivate him to return to his home. Their persistent efforts proved futile.

Billu did not feel very comfortable staying with his in-laws and wished to move into an independent accommodation. But, for fear of triggering off a social gossip, he decided not to move into any rental property in Jammu but instead move out of Jammu altogether.

For doing so, he needed to find a job outside Jammu. Working overtime and with a determined effort, he started sending job applications across the planet, mainly based on job ads. He also sent his resume to a number of his friends and relatives, which included his brother-in-law, Vijay Kaul, who lived in Malaysia. Towards the end of October 1994, as a permanent strategic move, Billu also applied for migration to Australia. As he and Rekha had no sponsors in Australia, the Australian High Commission assessed his application under the 'Independent Migration' category, ie. he had to prove that his credentials and technical qualifications met the Australian standards and the industry requirements to be able to obtain the migration visa. Being an engineering professional, he was asked to sit for the 'Test by Examination' conducted by the Institution of Engineers, Australia. The Test comprised two written examinations in various engineering subjects, three hours long each, over two days.

In the meantime, on Deepawali of 1994, Billu received an offer letter from a Malaysian Consultancy. At that time, Billu and Rekha were temporarily living with Bhaisahib and Mummyji. They had been living there for about a week. Billu's brother-in-law, Dr M L Pandit, arrived on his scooter one evening to hand over the letter. Billu was extremely thrilled to receive it. Although the offer was not very attractive, he decided to accept it.

For his employment, the Malaysian company had to first obtain his work permit from the Malaysian Immigration department, as also the dependant permit for his family. The process involved lengthy paperwork, mainly through facsimiles. As the facsimile facilities depended on the power supply, which were not very reliable in Jammu at that time, Billu decided to move to Delhi, along with his family. Initially, for the first two weeks, they stayed with Rekha's aunt and uncle, Dr Vijay Kachroo, at their home in Green Park. Dr Kachroo organised the facsimile facilities at a nearby ISD/STD/facsimile vendor. He would personally drive Billu twice, or sometimes thrice, a day to collect and send facsimiles to Malaysia to obtain the work visa. After all the paperwork was completed, Billu was advised by the company to wait for issuance of the visa. He was advised by the company that it could take up to two to three months.

As he did not want to return to Jammu, Billu went to live with Auntie. Billu tried to move into a rental accommodation nearby, but Auntie did not feel comfortable with that move for fear of any social gossip. She kept advising him to return to Jammu to his parents, which was the last thing on his mind. He found himself in a very precarious position. The family spent a few (uncomfortable) weeks there. During that period, Malaysian Airlines planes, flying overhead in their approach to the airport, teased him and tested his patience on a daily basis.

When it became too uncomfortable at his aunt's place, Billu moved to the Indian Institute of Technology, Delhi guesthouse. They also stayed for few days at the guest house of the Institution of Engineers, India. Billu needed a roof for his young family in Delhi till the arrival of the Malaysian visa. He was caught in a delicate limbo and constantly wondered what to do and where to bide time. The visa seemed to be taking forever and his patience started running thin. In the end, just before the visa arrived, the family stayed for one week in the vacant apartment of Rekha's younger sister.

After the arrival of the visa, Billu booked his tickets for Kuala Lumpur and, as a gesture of reconciliation, returned to his parents' home at Jammu, where he and his family stayed for about one week. His parents accompanied him to Delhi to see them off at the airport. On the evening of 26 January 1995, the Republic Day of India, Billu and his family left India and were seen off at the IGI Airport by Billu and Rekha's parents.

Before leaving Delhi, Billu informed the Australian High Commission in Delhi about the change in his circumstances. He also sent them a copy of his offer letter from the Malaysian company. The High Commission at Delhi advised him to contact the Australian High Commission at Kuala Lumpur on reaching there and provide them with his new contact details. Billu was undecided about living and working in Malaysia in the long term and returned to India several times in the next three years.

On 17 April 1997, the family boarded a Malaysian Airlines (MAS) plane to mark their initial entry into Australia. This was the first time that they were seated in a Boeing 747-400, which was the largest passenger plane in the world at that time. Eight hours later, after a brief stopover at the Melbourne International Airport, where most of the passengers disembarked, the plane took off for Adelaide. With a beautiful morning sun peeping through the right side windows of the plane and their destination being not very far, the family was very excited. The airline staff gifted two bags full of toys to both Baba and Deeksha.

Next day the plane touched down at Adelaide International Airport. An hour later, they arrived at their pre-booked, fully furnished, apartment at Burnside. It was a beautiful, second storey apartment. Thus began Billu's life in Australia.

# Cultural Transition & Challenges

> *Come, let's get drunk, even if it is our ruin,*
> *For sometimes under ruins one finds treasure.*
> —Hafez, (1325-26—1389-90)

> *Of what use will be a dish of roses to thee?*
> *Take a leaf from my rose-garden.*
> *A flower endures but five or six days,*
> *But this rose-garden is always delightful.*
> —Sa'di (1210-1292), Gulistan

## Changing Kashmir

In a landlocked place like Kashmir, it would not have been very easy for people to survive during harsh winter months, when not much food and energy would have been available to the common public. There must have been 'something' spiritually unique in the valley that it is said to have attracted Jesus Christ to travel and live there about 2,000 years ago; followed by Adi Shankaracharya a thousand years later and a number of well-known Sufi and Muslim saints from West Asia.

That 'something' was Kashmir's Shaivism, and its earlier forms, which was practiced by Kashmiri Pandits who are the original inhabitants of the valley.

After the arrival of Sufi and Muslim saints from West Asia during the last 500 years or so and during the reign of several alien rulers, a large number of people from the Pandit community converted to Islam. With time, Kashmiri spirituality comprised of a unique tapestry of Kashmir Shaivism and Sufism.

The perceivable difficult living conditions in the valley would have resulted in high interdependence and harmony amongst the people, with great reliance on the spirituality for treating physical and mental ailments. Logically, with time, spirituality would have woven itself well into Kashmiri thought, language and the food, producing a unique Kashmiri culture. Not surprising that Kashmiris are historically known for spirituality, adaptability, resilience, intelligence and hospitality. It seems, however, that her troublesome past, geographical isolation, a relatively harsh environment during the winter months with meagre resources, and a snail's pace in the post-1947 industrialisation and development, with a paucity of jobs, have all made a significant negative impact on the common Kashmiri psyche over the course of the last seven decades.

Kashmiri culture has roots in spirituality and Sufism. Like trees, if the roots are not nurtured, the consequences are unacceptable and reprehensible. The last few decades have seen a systemic erosion of the traditional Sufi values and tolerance in the valley, which has been accompanied with growth of extreme and fundamental versions of Islam.

Why did the West Asian Muslim and Sufi saints really come to Kashmir? Did they perceive the valley as *Reshvaer* (a garden of Rishis and Sages) or as a valley of infidels? Were they attracted to the valley due to its rich spirituality or they only intended to erode its spirituality and convert the people to Islam?

Religion and culture are two separate things and must not be confused with each other. Like Indonesia, most Kashmiri Muslims had Pandit ancestors before the Sufi saints had arrived from West Asia. Therefore, Kashmiris must learn from Indonesia, the largest Muslim country in the world, which has consciously preserved its original identity.

The national emblem of Indonesia is *Garuda*. The emblem *has* a heraldic shield on its chest and a scroll held by its claws. The shield's five emblems represent *Pancasila*, the five principles of Indonesia's national ideology. The wording on the scroll can be loosely translated as *Unity in Diversity*. Indonesians have not changed their traditional names to acknowledge, respect and preserve their identity and culture.

Unlike Indonesians, Kashmiri Muslims have not retained their traditional Kashmiri names. Even the historical (Kashmiri) names of numerous big and small towns have gradually been replaced with Islamic names, eg. *Anantnag* (endless/perennial spring) is commonly called *Islamabad*; *Umerheer* (*Umbar-heer*, ladder to the sky) is known as *Ahmad Nagar*; and *Reshvaer*, as Kashmir used to be known as, is now called by the locals as *Peervaar*. Even Pakistan has retained some original pre-partition names, eg. Haripur, Nankana Sahib, Lahore and Kasur (or Qasur) but not Kashmir.

As for the days of the week, except Friday (*Juma*), the names of all other days of the week have remained unchanged. Interestingly, *Battavaar* (Saturday), which has the word *Batta* embedded in it, has survived so far; so has the name of a locality called Batmalloo (or *Batamallo* or *Batamaalun*)! It is only a matter of time before the word *Batta* may be removed from these names, however.

## The Challenges

Kashmir currently faces three main challenges:

> Environmental and ecological vandalism undertaken by irresponsible, selfish and mindless elements of the

Kashmiri community, which seems to have accelerated after 1990.

A sharp and systematic erosion of the traditional Kashmiri values and culture, and introduction of alien cultures to replace them, which is driven systematically by the influential members of the community. It seems Kashmiris are consciously trying their best to shake off their historical roots and wear a new (alien) identity.

Political instability, which has been caused due to a number of factors, including sustained exploitation of the Kashmiri people by their political leaders on the directions of some external forces.

The first two issues present an existential threat to Kashmir and must be urgently addressed. Without its ecology and culture, Kashmir may cease to exist.

The third (political issue) can only be resolved through a sincere and sustained dialogue, and growth of mutual trust and goodwill. Finally, the onus is on the Kashmiri people; they must keep a cool head and in wisdom carefully analyse various international political scenarios and pick their best options. At the moment, it seems their heart is governing their prudence and common sense.

The Kashmiri people must pragmatically assess their neighbours in terms of:

Political stability;
Democratic and secular values;
Social fabric;
Prospects of a bright future for their youth;
Potential for positive contribution to the world at large;
Current and prospective economic strength; and
Current and prospective military strength.

Using religion as the sole criterion in their decision-making process is just not a prudent approach if they intend to bring everlasting peace to their people.

What Billu experienced recently in Kashmir (5 to 10 July 2016) shocked him to the core, yet again! Unfortunately, Kashmir seems to have well and truly become embroiled now in a *Catch 22* situation! What he saw in Kashmir does not make any sense, whatsoever, to any rational and peace-loving mind. He watched in absolute shock, disbelief and bewilderment how young children, as young as 10-years-old, attacked the security forces in the aftermath of a militant leader's (Burhan Wani) death. Children should either be studying in the school or playing, not fighting with the security forces! Similarly, the youth should either be studying or busy in the workforce.

Interestingly, when the 'educated' father of the slain militant was interviewed about six months before his death, he seemed to have been mentally prepared to see him killed (sacrificed) in the name of religion.

It is a pity and extremely unfortunate what these young Kashmiri children and youth are doing, or are being coerced/incited/motivated/inspired/encouraged to do, which is in a stark contrast to what their Pandit cousins are doing outside the valley. While the Kashmiri children and youth are seemingly being raised with hate, anger and violence and the youth seem to compromise and endanger not only their own futures but also their young lives, their Pandit cousins seem to focus, as always, on their education and, thereafter, coexist peacefully with the world community.

A number of simple questions have been haunting Billu since his return from Kashmir:

> Did the stone-pelting children really know what they were doing and why? Are these children really under the control of their parents or under the (remote) control of some people whom they may have never met? On whose behest do they act?
>
> Why do some elders and leaders of Kashmir instigate their youth to raid the camps of the security forces and attack

them with stones and sticks? Who does not know that it is sheer madness, rather suicidal, to try and snatch the weapons of the security personnel? Therefore, why do these elders and leaders instigate their children and the youth to commit suicide?

Is it a religious war rather than a political issue? If yes, what is the basis of the *religious war*? Who is infringing on the religious freedom of the Kashmiris, now that the Pandits have more or less disappeared? Aren't Kashmiris practically free?

The so-called political leaders have been crying long for *azaadi* but do they actually know the meaning of the word *azaadi*? Seemingly not! They must ask the Pandits what real *azaadi* means, as Pandits have tasted it after 1990.

It is abhorrent to get youth and children injured and killed. History will perhaps never forgive the real culprits after they are identified by the majority Muslim community; they bear the responsibility for compromising the lives and the future of their younger generations!

Since 1947, Jammu & Kashmir always has had a local government, dominated and driven by the members of the majority community from the valley. As a general experience, the members of the minority Pandit community were anecdotally disadvantaged and marginalised. For example, in 1948, a written examination (English and Mathematics) was conducted in Kashmir to fill up 17 positions of Post Masters. The results indicated that out of the top 17 successful candidates, 15 were Kashmiri Pandits.

Sensing that the results would displease the majority Muslim community, the results were not declared and the positions were not filled. After two years, a team from Delhi arrived to investigate into the matter. The old answer books were rechecked but the results remained unchanged. Subsequently, the Central government had to give in to the local state government's demand and considerable pressure for pleasing the majority Muslim community and preventing any political unrest in the valley, that the results be declared null and void. Soon afterwards, all 17 positions were filled, but with much fewer candidates from the minority Pandit community. Thereafter, this mindset became a precedence and the trend continued forever.

The Pandits did not fight for their rights or freedom or anything; they reconciled peacefully and, if they had a relatively thicker skin, they kept moving along with the mainstream. Those with a relatively thinner skin, however, would leave the valley without making any fuss and work very hard to re-establish in the wider world across the planet and try to provide their younger generation a better future. The trend continued till 1990 and the rest is history.

So, why can't the members of the Muslim community learn from their Pandit brethren and settle down peacefully for the sake of their younger generation? What is the problem in doing so? India has the third largest Muslim community in the world, as it has now overtaken Pakistan. If the members of the Muslim community can live peacefully and harmoniously in India, why can't the Kashmiri Muslims live like them?

Every Kashmiri must carefully think and sincerely answer one important question, 'Although Pakistan is an Islamic Republic, is it peaceful?' Similar is the case with Bangladesh and so many other Muslim countries around the world. In comparison to Muslim countries, isn't India a far more peaceful and tolerant country to live in? Aren't Kashmiris fortunate enough to live in a peaceful, progressive and strong India? The irony is that many people can't see that reality!

The branches of a tree, including the grafted branches, receive nourishment from the common roots of the tree. Similarly, for their peace, survival and growth, Kashmiris must look for their roots and nourish themselves with traditional Kashmiri values and spirituality. The roots of Kashmiri spirituality lie in Kashmiri Shaivism. The proponents and practitioners of Kashmiri Shaivism are Kashmir's Pandits. As such, it is very important for all concerned to recognise that the role of Kashmiri Pandits in Kashmir is to provide the present-day Kashmiris with a much needed connection with their original spiritual roots. Therefore, so long as Kashmiri Pandits don't return to Kashmir and reinstate the tapestry of Kashmiri culture and spirituality, return of peace to the valley is remote. Alien trees will never bear fruit in Kashmir; instead it is prudent to plant native trees.

It is another thing if the Pandits will now really be willing and prepared to return! If anyone actually decides to return, it will be a gift for the valley. The present inhabitants of the valley would do a great favour to their homeland by welcoming those Pandits.

Pandits are not, and have not been at the mercy of anyone; they chose to leave the valley out of their own volition and their decision to return to the valley will always be their own.

In Kashmir, they lived as peaceful, soft and gentle people. None of these terms reflects weakness; these terms reflect virtues, which were their strengths. To show one's strength, one does not have to carry a gun or a sword or shout abuse!

Contrary to what their Muslim brethren in Kashmir think about them, Pandits are not, and have never been, cowards. To save oneself from armed aggression is not cowardice; cowardice is to show aggression to virtuous and peace-loving people! Had Pandits been cowards, they would have surrendered their faith and converted to Islam. Instead, like their ancestors, they stuck to their roots and faith and opted for an unthinkable and brave option to leave their home. Cowardice is not saving one's life and honour in the face of an armed aggression; cowardice is to show aggression to unarmed peace-loving and virtuous people. It takes immense courage and guts to leave one's home behind and head out for an uncertain future. Their faith in themselves and their sustained hard work during the past quarter of a century has borne sweet fruit in time. They are well settled and continue to be peaceful and ever progressive, wherever they live on the planet.

It is extremely sad that some members of the Kashmiri Muslim community regard Pandits as a cancer and have unleashed a propaganda in the valley to target and scare away all remaining Pandits from the valley, as they previously did in 1989-1990, and, in the process, thwart the (unlikely) return of the migrant Pandits to the valley. Such individuals obviously don't have a clue about cancer and how it spreads. Had Pandits been a cancer, they would have infected all people amongst whom they lived on the planet, spreading violence and immorality across the world. Obviously, such has not been the case and Pandits are not involved in any violent or immoral act anywhere in the world. Clearly, such individuals in the valley are misleading their community and inciting them to do wrong things.

Given that the minuscule Pandit population in the valley cannot defend themselves or engage such individuals in any meaningful discussion, the onus is therefore on the whole Kashmiri Muslim community to contain such mischievous individuals and their cancerous and nefarious thoughts. Cancer must be contained so that the body survives.

Pandits may seem to have lost Kashmir but the rest of the world is their home now. The world has owned them and acknowledged their input.

One could say that Kashmir's loss has been the rest of the world's gain!

## Ecological & Environmental issues

The world-famous Dal Lake may potentially cease to exist in a few years. Its carrying capacity seems to have sharply dwindled due to:

> Unhindered reckless encroachment activities; and
> Mindless discharge of effluents into its waters from numerous houseboats and hotels around its periphery, which seems to have led to an alarming growth of weeds on its bed, as evidenced on its surface.

Dal Lake no longer appears to be as pristine as it once used to be. Dal looks more like a wetland, with densely populated weeds appearing over most of its surface area. Numerous ugly patches of localised red and blue algae can be observed in the nearshore areas. Reportedly, to a lesser or greater extent, similar is the case with Aanchar Lake and Wular Lake.

The *Char-Chinar* Island has unfortunately lost three Chinar trees and could be renamed as *Ek-Chinar*.

The River Jhelum and Doodh Ganga (used as flood channel) have significantly silted; both need urgent dredging works on a large scale to restore their original carrying capacity. If dredging is not carried out, the potential for future floods and their frequency significantly increases, with undesired outcomes.

Residential structures on the wetlands and the paddy lands are commonly visible. This has endangered the overall ecosystem and also reduced the land areas for the cultivation of crops. All construction activities must be immediately stopped.

Reckless deforestation and a sprawling residential/commercial development in the forest reserves have the potential to cause an ecological disaster. New trees, which are compatible with the local environment, must be planted in all patches where deforestation has occurred. A mushroom growth of commercial structures has taken place in the post-1990 period in Gulmarg and Pahalgam too. What is a tourist going to see there? If the authorities don't wake up soon and urgently put a stop to city development on forest land and wetlands, Kashmir may soon see numerous floods, cloud bursts and dry winters with high frequency. Sadly, it may not remain to be, as the world has historically known it to be, 'a Heaven on Earth'!

## Corrupt & Selfish

In the last half a century or so, widespread corruption has made its ugly inroads into Kashmiri culture, similar to the growth of a fast growing stubborn weed in Dal Lake. In many ways, the current surface of Dal Lake represents the current state of moral health in Kashmir.

To make things worse for the survival of Kashmiri culture, a sickly increasingly competitive social norm of acquiring and showing off material wealth and possessions, has come into existence between neighbours, friends and siblings, which has replaced the traditional Kashmiri modest thought. In a considerable number of cases, the women demand and their men provide, to keep them quiet and happy. This cycle of 'demands and supply' seems to have indirectly fuelled the rampant corrupt practices in Kashmir to acquire the extra, but undeserved, income.

Simple arithmetic indicates that most salaried people in Kashmir can't afford such big houses that can be seen everywhere across the valley or for that matter a number of houses, including the houses left behind by the Pandits; lavish weddings, gifts and the rich lifestyle based only on their monthly salaries. The additional money to feed their lavish and extravagant lifestyle must come from somewhere. Of course, easy come and easy go, as they say, but after taking a serious toll on the physical, political, moral and spiritual health of the individuals and the community as a whole. At the end of the day, no one is happy and satisfied. Is it all worth it? Not many people seem to care for the ecological and moral sustainability of their homeland.

It is worth noting that the corrupt practices by a considerable section of the community, who has traditionally been in power and by the people who are closely affiliated with the people in power, have left a sizeable major section of the Kashmiri community bareboned and disillusioned, which has increased their distrust and dissatisfaction with the government, and exposed them to exploitation by mischievous individuals. To sum up, the unhindered and rampant corruption has continued to feed the political unrest.

**Family Size**

The family size has now shrunk considerably. A few decades ago, a family's problem would be the problem of the whole *mohalla* (neighbourhood). The whole *mohalla* was the extended family. Be it a wedding or a death in a family, the whole neighbourhood, regardless of the religious divide, would come together and support the family. Nobody in the *mohalla* would need an invitation to attend a wedding or accompany a *barat* (a groom's wedding procession). All neighbours would participate and contribute quite informally! Even people of the adjacent *mohallas* would participate without invitation.

These days, a father and his married son, living in the same house, need to be invited separately, that too in person. If you really want them both to attend your function, you must invite them formally. A phone call or an email or an SMS will not do. We have now an intricate and complicated social structure, with increased self-importance of its individuals.

**Cultural Metamorphosis**

If Kashmiris consciously or unconsciously metamorphose into their alien/neighbouring cultures, by systematically replacing their traditional Pandit and Sufi values or their language or their food, Kashmiris will remain Kashmiris only in name. Here is an insight into the changing culture of Kashmiris, both in the valley and outside it.

The traditional Kashmiri virtues, such as simplicity and a modest lifestyle, seem to have now faded into the distant past. Instead, boisterousness and extravagance have taken over as the new order of the day. In the last few decades or so, a new cultural attitude of *manoo kee* (none of my concern) has become prevalent.

In the present times, self-interest generally governs a person's interaction with his extended family, friends and neighbours and the society at large. Kashmiris used to be prepared to sacrifice their self-interest to uphold the common ethical principles, but no longer. In the past, the older people in the *mohalla* would keep an eye on the younger people of the *mohalla* and quickly report to a family, if their son was seen smoking or in a cinema hall, or loitering around the streets after playing truant at his school. So was the case with unmarried girls, especially if she was seen walking with a stranger or at a place where she was not supposed to be. Now, if challenged, the younger people generally retort. Therefore, the older people prefer to turn a blind eye, which is not a healthy scenario in the broader sense.

With the passage of time and an improved geographical connectivity with the rest of the world, the cultural differences between Kashmir and her neighbours have dwindled remarkably. It is not surprising to observe that in a certain educated and elite class of Kashmiris, across the religious divide, families generally use a mix of non-Kashmiri languages (English, Urdu, Hindi) for communication, both at home and outside. It seems people suffer from an inferiority complex in speaking in the Kashmiri language, which, therefore, seems to have remained as the language of only the lower socio-economic class of the Kashmiri community.

In a worst case scenario, like the Sharda language, the spoken Kashmiri language may become extinct; it may only be a matter of time before that happens. The Śāradā or Sarada or Sharada script is an abugida writing system of the Brahmic family of scripts, developed around the 8th century. It was used for writing Sanskrit and Kashmiri. Originally more widespread, its use became later restricted to Kashmir, and it is now rarely used except by the Kashmiri Pandit community for ceremonial purposes. Śāradā is another name for Saraswati, the goddess of learning.

The affluent and the educated people are not providing a right direction to their communities! The people may be more affluent now, but they have also become time poor. Social interactions generally happen in the wedding season. It is obvious that social pressure has mounted disproportionately on relatively honest and poorer Kashmiris across the religious divide. Pandits wouldn't spend their wealth indiscriminately in the past, but lavish wedding receptions are a common sight now. It seems every family is in some kind of competition with the rest in showing off their wealth when performing the wedding ceremonies of their children.

In the older days, most marriages in Kashmir used to be arranged and would last for a life time. These days, a considerable number of young people choose their own partners. However, unfortunately, a significant number of those marriages fail soon after the wedding. In terms of marriage breakdowns, it seems the Pandits have caught up with the rest of world, in particular, the western world. Why is it so difficult to perform simpler weddings, save hard-earned money for use in a range of more sensible activities, such as (a) gifting it, or a part of it, to the newly wedded couple to kick-start their new lives; (b) save for one's old age and sickness; and (c) travel and see the world, have holidays?

The post-1990 era has seen an alarmingly increasing trend of inter-ethnic marriages. Whether we like it or not, the trend can't be reversed due to a much higher exposure of the Kashmiri youth to the other cultures. In the author's opinion, the diluting effects can be reduced only if the Kashmiri youth do not replace their original Kashmiri language with the non-Kashmiri language from their partners' side. One can always add another language but Kashmiris must not give up their mother tongue; more languages are better than one! A land is characterised by its geographical features and the people who live there. The people are characterised by their culture. If the thinking and behaviour of the people changes significantly, their culture is bound to change. And if that happens, it no longer remains the same place. No *zabaan* (language), no culture! No culture, no Kashmir; we may as well call her by any other name!

**The Food**

Kashmiris must also not replace their original Kashmiri dishes; howsoever, boring these dishes may taste or look to their children. Most importantly, at all costs, they must resist the temptation of fiddling and tampering with the ingredients (eg. spices) of our Kashmiri cuisine to make them cool. By doing so, the originality of the Kashmiri food will certainly be lost. As an example, none of the original Kashmiri Pandit dishes contains tomato, onion or garlic. If they want to add these things to any dish, then people should call that dish by some other name, so as not to mislead themselves, their children and the other people.

**Kashmiri Adaptability**

Based on their versatility and natural ability to fit in a wide range of situations and be compatible with alien cultures, Kashmiris are generally called *vaangun* (an eggplant or a brinjal). Their natural ability to quickly adjust to new environments, acquire a foreign language and cultural habits has historically served well all those Kashmiris who have migrated out of the valley during the last couple of centuries in their quest to survive. This ability is more or less akin to the chameleon characteristics of Kashmiris. The only problem is that, in the past, wherever the Kashmiris went to live, they held firmly onto their Kashmiri roots and did not replace their Kashmiri culture; however, today they don't hold on to their Kashmiriyat.

Tragically, a considerable number of Kashmiris believe that they may remain Kashmiris in name only, after a couple of decades or so. A question to them is, what are they doing to prevent it? In which direction are we moving at the moment? If at all there is a direction, we must consider if that is the right direction?

It is the author's sincere plea to all his Kashmiri brethren, Muslims and Pandits, that if we sincerely and honestly care for our homeland and want to serve her, we must rediscover our traditional culture, values and the virtues, before it is too late and diligently and consciously incorporate them in our youth and the children. In doing so, we must preserve our language and the traditional food.

It does not matter where we live; we can still play our role wherever we are. Most importantly, we must revive the traditional Kashmiri Sufi thought to nourish our roots and souls.

Is anyone listening or thinking?

**Dal-e-Bhatta**

In the pre-1990 era, the Pandit community was nicknamed as *Dal-e-Bhatta* (Pandits behaving like a *dal*), or *Dal-e-Gadva* (a pot of *dal*). It appears that, historically, for their survival in the Kashmir valley, being in the minority, the Pandits (also known as *Battas*) had to exhibit a fluid-like tolerance and resilience, like a deflated football, so the nickname. Interestingly, in the pre-1990 era, the Muslim community would consume much more *dal* (pulses), using it in a much wider range of cuisines than the Pandits. For example, unlike the Pandits, the Muslims would cook dal even with hard boiled eggs and meat. On an average, even though Pandits consume more meat than the Muslims and the Muslims consume more Dal than the Pandits, it is Pandits who are nicknamed *Dal-e-Bhatta*!

One has to understand that in Nature, there can be nothing as gentle and soft as air or water. Both sustain life. Soft and gentle do not mean weak. Seemingly, as fluids, both don't seem to have any strength to carry anything in their natural condition. But who does not know the power of wind and water when they move with purpose? Storms and floods destroy everything in their way.

There is nothing in the world that does not have elasticity, which means the ability of the material to deform under a certain stress. Young's Modulus of Elasticity is an important engineering parameter, which can be simply defined as the 'ratio of stress to the corresponding strain that it causes.' Even soils and rocks have their own degrees of elasticity to absorb loads imposed on them. Brittle materials crack and break under pressure. Therefore, in the engineering world, common construction materials, such as steel, concrete, plastics or rubber, all have elasticity to bend or twist or compress within the limits of their respective tolerances, which allows the materials to withstand the operational stresses.

Similarly, a person's strength must never be gauged based on that person's face or behaviour. Just because a person may naturally be gentle and soft spoken, or may appear to be so by enculturation, education and environment, does not mean that that person is necessarily a weak person. To summarise, the nick names of *Dal-e-Bhatta* or *Dal-e Gadva* for Kashmir Pandits must not be construed as the names for a weak community. Pandits have the natural tenacity, resilience and the flexibility to adapt successfully on a global scale to a vast range of environments and people, without causing harm to anyone. The Pandits are thinkers and thought always comes before the action; the world moves due to thought. As such, the Pandits will never be weak, as mistakenly claimed by their brethren in the valley. They will survive and continue to spread goodness all around.

**Broad Types of Kashmiris**

The Kashmiri men from both Pandit and Muslim communities can be categorised into the following broad categories. Some people may keep shuffling between these categories, as and when it suits their personal requirement, environment and the circumstances.

*Pragmatists*

These people are intelligent, demonstrate original thinking and want to get along with their lives without causing or getting involved in any fuss or controversy. They are generally rational in their thinking and practice a pragmatic approach to life in general.

Pragmatists go about their business without attracting much attention or distraction. Generally, they mind their own business and reveal any information only when you ask them. Their energies and attention remain mostly focussed on themselves and their immediate families. Judicious use of time is very important to them.

They keep themselves constantly updated with world affairs through books, newspapers and the news broadcasts. In political discussions, however, they remain apolitical to keep themselves away from landing into unnecessary controversial situations.

This category may comprise the bulk of Kashmiris, around 50 to 60 per cent.

*Sycophants*

These comprise people who generally sit on the fence and have no definite opinions of their own. These people rely on the common opinions of others, generally the majority. Their gossip thrives generally on the common rumours and hearsays. These days, for gathering their intellectual ammunitions for use in social settings, they rely mainly on the forwards that are posted by others on the popular social media or on popular news channels or the newspapers. In a group conversation, when people of fixed ideas discuss or argue on any matter, these people carefully ascertan the prevalent direction of the wind and who are the people in a dominating position in that social setting and at that point of time. After confirming the winning/ majority side, they can't resist chipping in with their two cents. Such people try their best to come across as quite gentle and learned people. In social settings, such people don't miss a chance to pass their opinion on 'all' matters of the world. These people never become leaders and can't be trusted as followers, because of their tendency to go with the wind, which is caused due to a serious lack of their personal convictions and scruples of their own.

Such people may comprise up to about 20 per cent to 30 per cent of Kashmiris.

### Leaders

These are people with ideas, generally fixed, with not much scope to move beyond those ideas. In Kashmiri society, such people used to be called *shodas*. Some people would also call them *mashaalis*, perhaps, they were seen as torch-bearers, ie. the people that carry a *mashaal* (a torch).

In the winter months in Kashmir, during a physical altercation on the road, they would generally hurl their hot *kangri* (a clay pot that contains burning charcoal and hot ashes) on the other person. At home, it is also not unusual to see such people throwing their food platter away during a serious argument with their spouse. Many such people throw even a radio or a television set out of their window if some news being broadcast is not to their liking, or if their favourite sports team loses. There are only two ways of dealing with such people: you listen to them with patience or you avoid them fully; there is no third way.

Such people comprise about 5 per cent to 10 per cent of all Kashmiri men.

### Chameleons

They are masters of quickly changing their colour and stealing your intellectual property. One needs to stay extremely careful in the company of and around such people. Such people usually lurk very close to you, as your close relatives or within your inner social circle, appearing to be your best friends. In doing so, they fully exploit your contacts and resources to their personal advantage. Using their mercurial ways, they generally succeed in avoiding your attention for a considerable time, and when you do understand them, it is too late. By then, you could have overinvested in your relationship with them. Thereafter, through emotional blackmail, they ensure you do not shun them, thus, ending up being your 'emotional vampires'. Such people comprise up to about 5 per cent to 10 per cent of all Kashmiri people.

Some vignettes of the typical Kashmiri mindset:

### Who is your Head of the Department?

The story dates back to 1980, when Billu was an undergraduate engineering student at REC Srinagar.

One day one of his relatives, who was an overseer (now called a Junior Engineer) in a state government engineering department, enquired about his Head of Department (HOD). Billu replied innocently that a certain Professor 'A' was the HOD. The relative then curiously asked about Professor A's qualification and Billu said the Professor had a Doctoral degree, in addition to Bachelor's and Master's Degrees in engineering.

On hearing this, out of jealousy, the relative made a sarcastic remark, 'Oh, I know him; his father was a compounder at a certain medical shop.'

It is important to note that this relative had only a diploma in engineering (not even a 'degree') and reportedly had failed several times earlier in his Matriculation (Year 10) examination.

This conversation provides an interesting glimpse of the mindset of a majority of Kashmiris.

Jealousy: Despite having a very poor academic record himself, the relative did not want to give Billu's professor any credit, whatsoever, for his academic and professional standing.

Professional bias: The relative did not think much about a compounder, although those days in Srinagar, several compounders would virtually run their own independent medical practices and were very popular with the public, such as Mohammad Shahban of Sathu Barbar Shah and Nannaji of Budhgair, Alikadal. People used to swear by them. Compounders have played an important role in the medical world.

This above mindset roughly indicates why class and caste system thrives even in this day and age.

### They don't need to know, it is between you and me

In 1997, Billu was working in Malaysia in a local engineering consulting industry. Through his persistent efforts and personal reassurances to the company, he had managed to find employment in his company for one of his friends, one Mr A, who had previously been his colleague in India. After a few months, Billu, on his yearly visit to India, also visited his previous workplace, where a number of his colleagues informed him that his friend, Mr A, had also moved to Malaysia and enquired if he knew about it or if he was in touch with him. He was surprised at their ignorance and innocently told them that Mr A was working very much with him in his company in Malaysia.

On his return to Malaysia, Billu asked his friend why he had not informed their colleagues in India about what had happened and how he had managed to move to Malaysia. To Billu's utter surprise, Mr A advised him, 'My friend, don't worry. This is a private matter between you and me; they don't need to know.' Billu replied, 'If you would have shared the news with others before coming here, maybe some other people, like you, would also have wanted to come over and work in Malaysia and I would have helped them as well.' That was true, as there was a gentleman, a common contact of Billu and Mr A, whom he had met in India, who had also been wishing to move overseas for work. Unfortunately, this gentleman did not know that Billu was working in the consulting industry, and not in the academic field.

The above story indicates a dark and extremely secretive nature of Kashmiri Pandits, which they may have developed over generations to survive in the Kashmir valley. This secretive character was profoundly demonstrated by Kashmiri Pandits during their mass exodus from Kashmir in early 1990. It is said that a majority of families moved out of Kashmir under the cover of darkness or very early in the morning, in extreme secrecy, during curfew breaks, without informing their relatives or their neighbours. It is also said that even siblings, living in the same house with their respective nuclear families, did not inform one another about their intentions to leave until all travel arrangements had secretly been made and a vehicle had arrived at their doorstep.

*Once again, don't tell anyone, it is a secret between you and me*
In December 2015, Billu attended the wedding ceremony of his friend's daughter. After the wedding, Billu asked his friend (Mr D) how much had it cost him?

In his turn, D asked, 'Including the cost of gold ornaments or without gold ornaments?'

Billu said, 'Excluding the cost of gold ornaments, as they are a gift to your daughter only, and will be an investment for her'.

D said, 'Please don't tell anyone. I am sharing this information with you in confidence. Well, including the gold ornaments, we have spent about Rupees 3.2 million over the last couple of years, but if you want to know our expenditure for the wedding ceremonies only, then the cost was around Rupees 2.5 million. The wedding reception alone cost us about Rupees 0.4 million. In addition, we had to pay for the hotel accommodation and food for the interstate guests that accompanied the groom.'

A worried Billu asked, 'My friend, what is going to happen to you? You have one more daughter to look after. After her wedding, you will be left a pauper. By the way, how did you manage to save all this money?'

Friend D said, 'It was not easy. We had to use all our savings and I also withdrew my Provident Fund to meet the expenses.'

He asked again, 'How will you manage your old age without savings after you marry off your younger daughter? Isn't it silly to spend so much money on the weddings? And, why did you have to pay for the hotel accommodation of the guests accompanying the groom? It would have been so much sensible if one joint wedding party was hosted by the two parties, with around 100 people attending from both sides. Both parties could then split the total expenditure.'

Mr D became a little restless and said, 'As the bride's father, in India, as per the custom it is expected that I should pay for their accommodation etc. If you were living in India, you would also comply with such societal expectations and do exactly the same as I have done.'

Billu asked, 'Is your daughter not educated and professionally at the same level as the groom? Haven't you worked very hard in bringing her up? Would you not wait for hours together, in rain and heat, outside her tutor's place? She is not inferior to the groom in any way. As the girl's father, in my opinion, your status should logically be considered higher than the groom's parents, but not lower in any shape or form. At best, she is equal to the boy, if not higher. After all, your daughter is going to be a member of the other family. In time, she is going to deliver their heir. People like you don't give your daughters the level ground and the status that they truly deserve.'

Mr D kept insisting that he was absolutely sure that Billu would also do the same thing as he had done, had he been living in India. Later, Billu calculated and made a rough guess that the total expenditure incurred may have been close to one million. Billu wondered why his friend had significantly inflated the cost! But it was not difficult to gauge why. It is a typical Kashmiri trait.

### I don't want trouble for myself

A Kashmiri Pandit, one Mr C, whom Billu had helped to find employment in his company, was posted full time at a construction site as the Company's Site Representative in Malaysia. His role, as the eyes and ears of the Company, was to closely monitor the quality of the work undertaken by the Contractor and make sure the work complied with the design intent and the relevant project specifications.

Billu was based in the Company's main office. He would visit the site at least once a week for his regular site inspections. During those initial site inspections, Billu would always be accompanied by Mr C. It so happened that during most of his site visits, Billu would spot some defective foundation piles. He would then go back to office and issue a Non-compliance Report (NCR) to the Contractor, along with recommendations for undertaking immediate remedial actions. Interestingly, Mr C never reported any non-compliance. After a couple of months, he noticed that Mr C had suddenly stopped walking with him

## Cultural Transition & Challenges 159

on the site. He would usually keep a distance of 20 to 30 m from Billu, much to the latter's wonder and curiosity.

One day, Billu asked Mr C, 'Why is that that I always spot defective piles during my site visits and you don't? There has not been a single report from you during the last two months. Also, why have you suddenly started to maintain a considerable distance from me when I walk around the site?'

Mr C replied honestly, 'The Contractor's Site Representative asked me last week if I was the person who had issued all those NCRs? I said to him that I am not the person; it is the other person who visits the site once a week for the site inspections. Look, I don't want any trouble on the site due to me. If I raise issues with the work, the Contractor may complain to the Company about me and the Company may remove me from the site. I don't want to lose the job.'

The above story illustrates a strange character of Kashmiris. A person is paid to do a job but in order to avoid becoming a focus of attention of the authorities, that person makes some compromises with the role. The character is based on the inherent psychological insecurity of some Kashmiris, which is interwoven with an element of distrust for another person who may have originally helped the first person.

*Maharah, I have not attained anything yet, how can I meditate?*
In 2005, a newly married Kashmiri Pandit, in his mid-thirties, about six-seven years younger than Billu, had regularly been sending out group emails to many people. The emails carried a spiritual message of a certain Godman, sometimes more than one email a day. Even in the social settings, he would mostly speak about spirituality and give sermons to other people about how life should be lived. Given to believe that the person was highly spiritual, Billu asked him one day over phone if he practiced some kind of meditation or yoga, to which this person replied in the negative. On hearing this, Billu wanted

to probe further and asked him some simple questions about the general philosophy of life and his personal view about some general aspects of life. Instead of replying directly, this person kept on referring to the Godman's preaching. But Billu did not give up and persisted about knowing this person's independent understanding about those aspects of life.

Finally Billu said, 'My dear, Swamiji's preaching are published in numerous books and are available on the internet. I would like to hear from you about your thoughts, not Swamiji's. If you don't meditate and contemplate, how do you give sermons to people about what should they do and how should they live, without having your own understanding? Now that you seem to be a keen student of spirituality, why don't you learn to mediate and contemplate? I can help you. Why don't we meet on a suitable day and I could teach you how to meditate.'

Finding himself cornered and exposed, this person said, 'Maharah (respected one), you are well settled in life; you have reached a high position in your profession; you own a house; have a car; and your children are doing well at school. I have nothing at this stage; I am just starting my life and I have a lot of work to do. How can I meditate and spend time in spiritual pursuits?' On hearing this, Billu immediately changed the topic of their conversation. The telephone chat ended on a cordial note. However, thereafter, this person never sent another group email to Billu. In all their future social gatherings, this person remained cautious and never gave sermons to other people in Billu's presence.

# Conversations in Wilderness

*We are the hollow men,*
*we are the stuffed men.*
*Leaning together*
*Headpiece filled with straw. Alas!*
*Our dried voices, when*
*We whisper together*
*Are quiet and meaningless*
*As wind in dry grass*
*Or rats' feet over broken glass*
*In our dry cellar.*

*Shape without form, shade without colour,*
*Paralysed force, gesture without motion;*
*Those who have crossed*
*With direct eyes, to death's other Kingdom*
*Remember us-if at all-not as lost*
*Violent souls, but only*
*As the hollow men*
*The stuffed men.*

—T S Eliot (1888–1965)

> *Out beyond ideas of wrongdoing and right-doing,*
> *there is a field. I'll meet you there.*
> *When the soul lies down in that grass,*
> *the world is too full to talk about.*
> *Ideas, language, even the phrase each other*
> *doesn't make any sense.*
>
> —Rumi (1207 –1273)

This chapter includes a series of general conversations that have taken place since January 2015, which marked 25 years of the exodus of Kashmiri Pandits from Kashmir, between Billu and people from Pandit and Muslim communities from Kashmir, on a popular social media interactive application. The conversations provide a snapshot of the kind of conversations the people of a certain educated and professional category among Kashmiris undertake today.

It must be noted that the conversations, and the topics discussed, cannot and must not be considered to completely represent the entire cross-section of all ethnic Kashmiris globally or all people from the two communities, Kashmiri Hindus and Kashmiri Pandits.

## MUSLIM FRIENDS
### Abdul Rasheed

Abdul Rasheed comes from a well-educated family in Srinagar. He is a very sober, sensitive and spiritual person, gifted with a high intellect and extremely high moral conduct.

Abdul Rasheed and Billu know each other since 1979. They worked as colleagues for nearly five years. A similarity in their basic individual nature and a shared common philosophy towards the world in general has made them good friends. Abdul Rasheed was present at Billu's wedding. They had the following conversations between April and November 2015.

*May 2015*
Billu: Dear Abdul Rasheed sahib, spent a few hours with you in my dream last night. You hosted me and my family and took us to an amazing and strikingly beautiful, but narrow, valley, with beautiful coloured structures on the slopes of the valley. God bless. Hope you are fine.

Abdul: Sorry for responding late. In fact, I had been out of station to Kishtwar for a site visit. I was tired last night. Regarding your dream—yes it has a connection. For the past twenty days, I have been feeling like telling you something very important but didn't understand what stopped me. Believe me I am convinced about your dream. Insha'Allah, I will be in touch.

*June 2015*
Abdul: Adaab. Hope you are well. (Has forwarded an article.)

Billu: Adaab, thank you. By God's Grace, all well on this side. Dad is here these days, so have been busy. How about you?

Abdul: Good. Take care of him. Spend as much time with him as you can. Parents are treasures. Well, I am fine Alhamdullilah.

Billu: *There is nothing noble in being superior to your fellow men. True nobility lies in being superior to your former self.*

—Ernest Hemingway

Abdul: Caste will be irrelevant when idol worship becomes irrelevant.

Billu: Exactly, all religions promote idol worship in one form or the other. Religious symbols and structures symbolise idol worship at micro and macro levels. The world is increasingly getting divided, unfortunately, and this will cause the ultimate doom of mankind. Looks like, as everything else, it is Almighty God's Will! As for me, I will continue to love His creation (man) in any shape, form, colour, religion and size that He has created. Without His Will, various religions would not have been born.

I am a herbivore and don't consume even dairy products. In my opinion, causing pain to even the animals, howsoever minor, is not right. Does it mean that my parents and all my ancestors, who consumed animal food, are, or were bad people? Absolutely NOT! Should I force my belief and thoughts on others? Absolutely NOT! I believe in the absolute free will of the man, as long as he or she does not infringe on the freedom of others, either physically or spiritually. Nature has created so many colours. Humans come in a range of colours, shapes and sizes too. We MUST NOT judge which one is right. That would be challenging HIS design. That applies to an individual's religion too. Religion is a personal matter of an individual and we must leave it there. Persecution, discrimination and killing of an individual based on his religion and gender, colour etc. is absolutely sinful.

Abdul: The article was more an analysis of social problems in India. What I believe is nobody in India is following his religion in letter and spirit. In fact, majority of people have not read their respective religious scriptures. We have left it to a few group of people who themselves also do not know it but are experts in making a fool of us.

Billu: Precisely, man has become highly materialistic. Most people pray either out of fear or, as insurance, for their personal material gratification. Having said that, I am sure, a small number must be praying for the love of God and for Self-Realisation, as should be. I left India but, as destiny has it, I come across such people (from that country) here also (in Australia) and their thinking has not changed. I am sure many such people are scared of me (due to my simple thought and lifestyle). Many such people possibly don't like me for my world citizenship and impartial thought, and because I don't follow the popular thought. All I can do is to shut up and try to keep my consciousness clean and surrender to His Will. Let Him give everyone wisdom and noble thought.

Abdul: I understand, as I am also feeling suffocated. But Alhamdulillah, I have read the Qur'an and, as such, I don't allow anyone from my community to ride upon me. It took me ten years to understand my religion. Tragedy in India is: all including intellectuals (with small exceptions) follow only one principle, 'whether my nation is right or wrong, I will follow it.'

Billu: He will look after us also in a manner He looks after the whole Universe. Let us surrender to His Grace!

Bhaijan, like millions and millions of Indians or Australians, I have also not deeply read religious scriptures. I believe in oneness and omnipotence, omnipresence, omniscience of God but I am NOT particularly religious. My personal religion is NON-VIOLENCE. I do respect all earthly religions and consider these more like universities, which MUST make us humans and teach us to be humane towards all other earthly beings. I believe in mutual love and universal brotherhood. I wish and pray there were more people like me.

Man (both man and woman) has a lot to fight against. Internally, man must fight his/her personal moral corruption, greed, lust, anger etcetera. Externally, using non-violent means, man must fight and overcome hunger, disease, illiteracy, gender inequality and poverty. In my opinion, if man has not understood this simple purpose of life, and does not follow it in letter and spirit, he/she has not yet graduated (from the university called 'religion'), Bhaijan, I have nothing more to add. I am a simple person, with a simple mind. Forgive me if you are not happy with anything I have shared with you about myself and what I believe.

Abdul: Very good morning! My dear, there is nothing wrong anywhere with you and me. I didn't carry on the chat on the previous topic because of paucity of time. I know you well. You don't have to describe yourself. In fact, I had mailed you the previous link because I found the article somewhat different and wanted you to analyse it socially. But I later understood, I should not have. But the intention was not to hurt your religious sentiments. We have been forbidden to do so. I am sorry. I know you're different from others. Take care.

I am just back from morning payers and want to sleep. Good day.

Billu: I am extremely apologetic for appearing to react to your earlier email. I did not mean to react. Forgive me. My emails only provided me with a vent to share my feelings and personal beliefs with you. If you again read my SMSs, you may realise the state of my mind, what I am going through, how sad, desperate and helpless I feel in this present world. I am not religious. I consider myself as a world citizen. Again, forgive me for any misunderstanding caused due to my SMSs. I only meant to open my heart to my elder brother.

Abdul: But what is the problem with your previous SMS? I didn't smell anything. It was normal. You have a right to express yourself, especially to me. Take care. Birds of the same feather flock together because there is something in common.

*July 2015*
Abdul: Adaab. Hope you are all well. I was tightly scheduled for the whole month of Ramzan. There was hardly any time to relax, breaking fast after more than 16 hours, getting free from night prayers at 11.30 pm and then getting up at 2.30 am again for *sahri* and then office during day time. Thank ALLAH, everything went smoothly and let us hope finally ALLAH accepts all this. Hence could not chat with you in detail. Anyway how are you all? Where is your father these days? Has he returned to India?'

Billu: Adaab and good morning. May you always be peaceful and healthy! My father returned to Delhi on 19 June. He flew to Srinagar on 23 June and then returned to Jammu on the Eid Day. He may return to Srinagar in the first week of August. Take care of yourself and be cheerful.

**October 2015**
Abdul: Forwards a popular social media post about '*Dadri killing*'.

Billu: Extremely unfortunate and repelling! We see various minority communities regularly being targeted in the Indian subcontinent, be it Kashmir, Pakistan, Bangladesh or India. For the last quarter of a century, I haven't been able to understand why some humans are victimised based on their religious beliefs, although people try to justify these dastardly acts from a range of political perspectives.

Last Friday, a 15-year-old Muslim boy in Sydney, inspired by the ISIS, shot dead a complete stranger in broad day light, soon after the Friday prayers. The victim was a 31-year-old white cop. Shame, but whose?

After the above tragic incident, there was not even a single statement from our PM or any other minister. The incident was treated as a regular crime and is being dealt with by the police. The local community is highly concerned but angry. Thankfully, there has been no reaction from anyone.

Abdul: For me, Pakistan or Bangladesh had no existence before India. I never used to define them with India but you have rightly brought India to their level. Another woman got gang-raped today. And another *Sahitaya Academy* award winner just returned her award after thirty years, in protest.

Billu: It is a jungle out there. A considerable number of so called humans are not actually humans. They are sub-animals in the garb of humans. Even animals must be feeing appalled. Not to speak of women, even men like me don't feel safe in the Asian countries, particularly the subcontinent.

Abdul: Very sad that humans are killing humans. The Sydney incident is equally disturbing. But it is an incident by an individual and may be called as a crime. While in India, mobocracy is taking over democracy. Religious beliefs are being forced upon with *goondaism*, with the tacit support of state machinery.

Billu: Just try to see the world from my eyes and you may get some idea about how I feel. For possible pain in the cows during milking, I became a complete herbivore (vegan) about three years ago. I feel very distressed when some humans behave as sub-animals and cause pain and death to other humans. Two rationalists were murdered in the last two months by Hindu mobs—one of them a professor. It was painful. I am not scared but it is painful the way India is shaping up under the new dispensation over the past one year. Honestly speaking, India was a beautiful country. You don't know it—I have watched this country during my formative years. And I tell you, bad days are ahead if the present dispensation does not change its mindset. God has to do justice at some point of time.

India is no different than Kashmir where half a million strong KP community was targeted by the armed representatives of the majority community about 25 years ago. No one has apologised and taken responsibility so far. Some of those armed representatives are prominent present-day politicians.

Abdul: Now does it mean that since Kashmiri Pandits suffered in Kashmir during militancy and no murderer apologised for it, so the lynching of Dadri Muslim is justified? I think you're getting the chat politicised—that is where we are actually. By the way, during those bad days, I tried to reach out to all those non-Muslim near & dear ones whom I could. So much so, on two occasions I was heckled by two of them in

Jammu-Delhi—one was my very close friend here—interesting isn't it. Any way, you have drifted the whole chat out of track.

No further disturbances for you—last chat. My first chat was an expression of pain to some select people. Most of them were my class fellows at Chandigarh—one Jammu'ite and you—all likeminded. But I understand you got offended and that was not the intention. I never wanted you to apologise for the gruesome killing. Apology should come from those who are behind the mobocracy. Alhamdulillah, you and I are both noble souls. Sorry for keeping you engaged for long and perhaps you felt tortured through your wrong mathematical interpretations. May ALLAH bless both of us and all.

Billu: I am quite surprised to learn about your diplomatic inference of my words, considering you know me well. I could be anything but a diplomat. I am well known for being very direct. Every living being is dear to me and I feel immense pain when any living being gets killed due to any inhumane act of a so-called man, for whatever reason. I was devastated recently when Cecil the lion was lynched by an American dentist in Zimbabwe. Two wrongs don't make one right, be it Kashmir or UP. If I was an Indian, I should hang my head in shame at what happened in Dadri. If I was an Indian Hindu, I should do the likewise. I have emigrated long ago due to the tragic reasons that are known best to you. However, I feel very sad to see my erstwhile home in such a sorry state.

It is the responsibility of the local government in UP to keep every citizen safe. They have failed. The culprits must be taken to task. But will they? Only God can help, as I have the least expectations from any man. Since 1947, after the British left, India has been governed by regimes who continued the policy of 'divide and rule'.

I am not sure whether you are upset, angry or just busy. My request to you, as your younger brother, is to learn meditation and then meditate regularly. I have been practising meditation since 1991. It has helped me to reconcile and forgive people. One thing you must remember, and that is 'Mother Nature resets everything'. She never forgets anything. Take my word—Mother Nature will have the last laugh, as always. BTW, during my last visit, I noticed Kashmir may be on the path of ecological and environmental suicide. Reckless people have constructed massive residential and commercial structures on wetlands, paddy lands and forest reserves. Kashmir has a delicate ecology, unlike Rajasthan. So, we must watch out for floods, cloud bursts, forest fires, landslides and earthquakes. Have a nice day.

Please transcend, do not limit yourself. God is one! Without His Will, there would not have been humans born to the other religions and sects, major or minor. You need to love and pray for Muslims and non-Muslims alike. All are dear to God. Khuda hafiz!

*May 2016*
Billu: Dear Rasheed sahib. I am writing a book related to my memoirs on Kashmir and my Kashmiri friends. I intend to reproduce our chat in the book and address you as Abdul Rasheed in my conversation for the book. The time, date and contents of our conversation remain unchanged. I hope you have no objection to my doing that. My best regards and love for you and your family.

Abdul: Adaab. I am fine and I hope you are also well. I did receive your message yesterday but to be more precise I didn't get time to go through it. I was very busy during the day and back home I was tired, with a lot of structural fatigue. If I am more honest, perhaps I didn't have the appetite also to go through your message. I am cautious.

Regarding your second part—about writing a book, I don't know what is in your mind. You are within your rights to do whatever you feel like. Honestly, I don't have any interest in politics, neither do I adore political people. My structural engineering is my second religion and I love learning it day by day. Please don't take any other meaning out of this message. I don't like debating on issues where I can't contribute anything. May ALLAH keep you happy. Take care. Thanks for your message.

Billu: Adaab, thank you for your message. I feel really obliged. My book has no political intention, as I am practically a foreigner. It is a family memoir. We'll lose it if I don't document it. I also hope it will help to stitch the two communities back together. I have tried to highlight the best of both communities before and after the migration and their interdependence and where Pandits are now? You will enjoy reading it, I hope. My best regards to you and your family.

Abdul: As I told you, these topics don't create any interest for me.

## Sajid Khan

Sajid Khan is a specialist medical doctor. He has spent most of his adult life overseas in the US. He is an intelligent, conscientious and sensitive person. The following conversation occurred between March 2015 and May 2015.

### March 2015

Billu: How unfortunate (on receiving a forward from someone else).

Sajid: Is this an editorial or a letter from a reader? I can sense a stupid mind behind this writing.

Billu: This is an open letter in circulation. A close Muslim friend of mine received it from his cousin. Seems to be preparations for a repeat of Jan 1990! Well, what can one do? It is extremely unfortunate. Some people don't want Kashmir to return to peace!

In the open letter, the author calls non-Muslims as infidels. So, in this context, the definition of an infidel would also be a 'God loving, God fearing, peace loving, non-violent, Kashmiri Bhatta'! Why do these people still want to murder the remnant Bhattas? Would that give them *azaadi* ? From whom? *Bhattas*? Are Bhattas still a hurdle to *azaadi*? Even a 5-year-old can ask this question. But who can answer? No one!

Sajid: I think, as you are well aware, this is a complicated and deep issue. I have my feelings and personal experiences on this subject. My father and my family have personally experienced the pains of this issue. On the web, I found the founder of this party. I have no regard for someone like him. This I say based on personal knowledge. Also, I have some knowledge of other leaders involved. Most of which is not positive. But mostly, I cannot claim to have complete knowledge of all the issues, eg. I don't know the exact reason why Kashmiri Pandits left Kashmir so suddenly and all at once. I do believe some of them received threats because of some reasons. But, do we (you and me) believe that the whole Pandit community was in danger? I don't know the answer to that. I can believe some individuals could have been, because of their involvement.

I personally believe Kashmir has lost by the loss of the Pandits. A large part of the Kashmiri culture and everything good is a direct contribution of the Pandits. Most of my teachers have been Pandits. I have personally learnt many good habits from them and not just book knowledge.

I wish you had met and had a chat with my father. Well, you and I haven't met yet. Hopefully soon! I spent a brief but good time with your dad recently and I cherish that much. Hopefully, I have more such opportunities.

Billu: One lakh KP families may have one lakh stories. Mass migration happened between 20 Jan 1990 and June 1990. I left

Kashmir originally in Oct 1989, but came back for a few weeks and then finally left in December 1989.

Well before the mass migration, between April 1989 and Dec 1989, due to random but frequent violent incidents in the valley and my strong awareness of the undercurrent and the forthcoming onslaught, I suffered severely due to high anxiety and depression. I had a strong feeling that something was very wrong, not good vibrations in the environment. My feelings proved right a few months later. My wife would accompany me to the REC and wait for me in the Hazratbal Shrine for those two to three hours during which I would take my classes. This continued for three weeks at a stretch in December 1989. No one believed my fear and sensed my feelings. I constantly feared for my life and for my family.

My parents and my cousin left the valley on 20 Jan 1990. On the historical day of 19 Jan 1990, my dad was touring Kokernag, which was an active area of the militancy at that time, but we did not know. That night, his Kashmiri Muslim boss and boss' younger brother repeatedly called my home and strongly urged my parents to leave for Delhi for a month or so. Perhaps, they knew what was happening and probably going to happen. They wanted to save the lives of my parents. My maternal uncle left Kashmir about a year after the mass exodus of the Pandits. He received repeated death threats from some militants. My wife's great uncle (Maheshwar Nath Bhat Gosani) was shot dead by militants in his home at Lal Mandi, along with his personal assistant. He was around 70 years old at that time.

As I said, there are at least one lakh stories out there. You should individually ask individual people from the Pandit community.

We felt betrayed by both the Indian government and our fellow Kashmiri brethren. Before I escaped, the faces of my colleagues at the REC had changed significantly. Many of my colleagues had been my classmates and close friends. I still meet them. But at that time, the warm, loving smiles and warmth in their hugs and handshakes had suddenly disappeared.

I was baffled and wondered what had happened to them? They would avoid talking to me. What did they know that I did not? Hindsight, they probably thought that, like others, I was also a sacrificial sheep, destined for slaughter. It still pains me. I lost my home and heritage. A permanent loss!

While you may consider returning to Kashmir one day and spend a predominant part of the year in the valley, I don't have the same freedom and luxury. I may be allowed to visit my relatives there, but I may not be allowed to live and settle back there. This open letter by this organisation bears a testimony to my feelings. I am branded an infidel. Can you imagine that? Do you really believe that I don't love and fear God?

Very unfortunate things have happened, and will sadly continue to happen. My eyes are full of tears, as I write this note to you. What was my fault?

Sajid: I can feel your pain. And I grieve with you, as I would for my own brother. Our family was raised differently. I grew up innocent of hatred, especially religious. Most of my friends in school were non-Muslims. I have gone to many temples and gurdwaras in Kashmir and do so even now here in my town. I have participated in Diwali Pooja several times. I take great pride in our relationship. That's who I am and that's what I teach my kids. Unfortunately, voices of reason get muffled most of the times.

Billu: …I wonder about this world. I turned into a vegetarian when I was a three-year old—I can't even bear the pain of the animals, not to speak of my fellow human beings. What use is freedom if that freedom is attained at the cost of the lives of my fellow human beings, irrespective of who they are? Aren't all humans the children of the same, one and the only one, God? If He nourishes us all, why do we harm one another? I am baffled and sad.

Sajid: Alas, if only more of us could understand this simple concept, we would be living in a much happier world. We'll get there one day, but after much pain and suffering! Always happy to hear from you!

I keep looking forward to your messages. We should try very hard to meet and spend some time together.

May 2015

Sajid: Aadaab. I enjoy our exchange. Just caught up in the rigors of life! Close to the end of the school year here, with kids' events and all. We are well, thank Allah. I have heard many nice things about you and wish to meet you soon.

(After seeing a video) I hope I never have to see any mom, sister or daughter that I know of do this in/for public.

Billu: Kashmir has changed forever. How many people in Kashmir speak in Kashmiri? Most Kashmiri children speak either in Urdu (in the valley) or Hindi (outside the valley). As a race, we suffer from 'inferiority complex'!

Sajid: I have a choice to not be part of this change.

Billu: We too! Our first language was practically English. Since 1998, we consciously choose to speak in Kashmiri at home. Both our children speak reasonably good Kashmiri. Our food remains what our ancestors ate, except I have chosen to be an herbivore. Proud to be a Kashmiri! It is debatable how many KPs will now return to the valley (perhaps a few hundreds) if the government sincerely works on their return. In my opinion, when a house loses its soul, it should be abandoned. KPs must forget the valley and recreate pieces of Kashmir wherever they live on this planet. No issues. I will say the last line slightly differently in today's context—Live, Love & Let Live!

Sajid: True.

**Asif Ahmad**

Asif Ahmad and his wife, both medical doctors, are academically gifted and have been high achievers. They live and work in the UK. The following chat took place in January 2015.

Billu: Greetings, Asif sahib, just received it (a video clip) and I thought I should share with you. You must have been a very young child then. I had already 'escaped' from Srinagar for fear of our lives and honour, first in Oct 1989 and eventually on 23 Dec 1989. On that day, I had decided to spend the night at the airport itself if I did not get flight tickets. My parents and my cousin Sapna escaped on 20 Jan 1990 after my father's Muslim boss and his younger brother vehemently urged my parents to leave the valley. Rest is history. Very bad things happened 25 years ago. Scars and bad memories remain. Pray it remains only a thing of the past and never gets repeated.

Asif: Regards! I can feel the pain and sufferings of the Pandit community arising due to the mass exodus. Kashmir and all Kashmiris, irrespective of whether they are in or outside Kashmir, are suffering ever since. I am sure there are many of that generation who want to return. Although my knowledge is insufficient I think things are much deeper than what they appear to be. Look what is happening around the world this time. It is difficult to believe what is true and what is not.

My best friends are from the Pandit community. We were in the same school together when they left to join colleges outside the state. I am sure many people like me had friends and neighbours who regarded them more than their own family. It is impossible to believe how that spirit and sense of oneness can vanish overnight and turn friends into enemies...impossible!

As people who believe in equality and justice, I am sure you will agree with me that any wrong doing by any Kashmiri or for that matter any person on this earth doesn't go unaccounted for....that is the law of nature! I am sure people who have done wrong to any member of the Pandit community have been brought to justice. Same way, in the name of justice, it is important that we speak about mass rapes and millions of orphans suffering silently and there is no one to speak for them.

I think Kashmiris who left or those who are still there are two faces of the same coin, you can't separate them. One has no value without another. It is important that we understand this sooner until it is too late.

Forgive me if I have written anything wrong. I know you are someone who is not an emotional, unreasonable thinker. That is why I took some liberty to pen down some of my thoughts.

May be we could spend some more time on the subject when you visit us. Haven't watched the video yet! Regards.

Billu: I appreciate your sentiments. The contents of your message are reasonable and valid. I share your concern and pain due to the current world scenario. Lately, I have started questioning God's (worst) creation, i.e. man!

Are the humans, Mother Nature's greatest blunder? Humans devour everything on this planet, including their own kind, for greed and lust. We are the most dangerous species on the planet. How long will Mother Nature tolerate us? God bless you and your family with good health and happiness.

Asif: I agree. Man has been created as a vicegerent on this earth, and is described as 'best of the creations'. It is unfortunate that we are ashamed of being humans. Anyways, this has always been there.

Billu: (Forwards a poem)—Nice lines.

Asif: A lovely poem...summarises life and its realities. The poet must have been in real depression.

Billu: I have known the message of the previous video all along my life, since I was a 3-year-old child. In my life, I never have had to refer to any literature or a religious book/script to know what is right or wrong. To me, and millions like me, God is omnipresent, like $H_2O$ (water), even in rocks. God is in each one of us and we are all in God. Only our individual egos and thoughts separate us from one another. Without God's will nothing happens. Even non-believers (atheists) are also due to His/Her Will!

For me, *insaniyat* (humanity) and *ahimsa* (non-violence) are the highest religion. The barbaric (terrorist) acts around the world, including those in Pakistan recently, cannot be justified by any argument. No religion allows it. Then why do those happen? Why do people misuse their religion and under its garb try to gain power and control others? On its own, no religion makes its followers good or bad! Religion plays no role! It is only misused!

Asif: Dear brother, you have hit the nail on its head. Religion should not be blamed for someone's craziness. If a Jew, Christian or a Hindu kills someone, why do people of so called reason and intelligence blame Christianity, Judaism or Hinduism? Look at what happened to Babri masjid or in Gujarat? Men of reason and justice are now ruling the country.

I believe man is here for a reason, like the Sun; everything living or non-living has a reason. It is for us to find it out and that's where religion comes. It cannot be learnt from any mortal method.

I agree, the greatest religion is humanity and to treat everyone with respect and equality. I will send you the English translation of the Khutbah/sermon that Prophet Muhammad (peace be upon him) delivered at the time of his last Hajj pilgrimage. Regards

## A KASHMIRI PANDIT TM GROUP
*December 2015*

Billu: I am starting today a series of messages loaded with Bhaisahib's teachings to me. Although the recipients of this message may also possibly have received similar instructions from Bhaisahib, I thought I should share my treasure with you.

The first and foremost rule of the TM is: Keep it simple.

Bhaisahib taught me the true meaning of *Satyam Shivam Sundram*. A 'truth' (not 'the truth') which causes pain and strife is not 'the truth'.

### New Year 2016

Faith and trust in your Deity and the Guru must be absolute, ie. 100 per cent. In TM, we have been given a torch in our hand and finding our way forward is our responsibility. We must not waste this opportunity.

### Guru Days January 2016

Adi Sankara emphasised the importance of love to achieve the ultimate liberation.

During these Guru Days, we must not forget to pray for eternal peace of Guru Tegh Bahadur ji, without whose supreme sacrifice, perhaps we would not have been what we are at the moment.

### Women's Day Jan 2016

The understanding of the Creator should be 'through' His/Her Creation.

Bindroo A K: (Forwards a post about women) Till the day she dies, everything she does... cooking, cleaning your house, taking care of your parents, bringing up your children, earning, advising you, ensuring you can be relaxed, maintaining all your family relations, everything that benefit you, sometimes at the cost of her own health, hobbies and beauty. So who is really doing whom a favour? Dear men, appreciate the women in your lives because it is not easy to be a woman. Happy Women's Week! A salute to all the ladies!

Billu: A society can't be called emancipated and developed if the female gender is considered as relatively inferior to the male gender and/or considered as a commodity that can be given away. Having said that, we need to closely scrutinise the term *kanya-daan* (it means symbolic donation of a daughter at her wedding) and decide if it is fair, valid and justified. Who gives us the right to 'donate' our daughters? She is not a commodity! She is at least equal or better than her male counterpart in all respects. Don't we see the Mother Goddess in her? Let us all think deeply!

Do we have the courage and the will to review and amend this outdated terminology of *kanya-daan* and the religious practice of seemingly donation of our daughters at their wedding, as the term suggests?

### Trees and Humans Jan 2016

When a seed is sown in the ground, a plant grows if the soil is fertile enough and if the seed gets adequate sun, water and care from the gardner. Sometimes, the plant becomes a tree but only if it continues to grow well. A tree contributes significantly to the world in numerous ways. Every tree gives back something. Trees absorb carbon dioxide and produce oxygen during daytime. Some trees provide *shehjaar* (cool shade) and nesting shelters to birds, and some bear delicious fruit. When nothing is left to be given, trees are sometimes cut. Some trees provide firewood and some timber for the construction of houses, furniture, etc.

Like trees, when we get initiated into TM, our Guru (the gardner) sows a seed in us.

### Contemplation Jan 2016

Subash: None of us knows anything to be precise...whatever comes out spontaneously is written and nothing more... The crux is *Dhyaan Karo...aur Kertey Raho...*(meditate and continue to remain in a meditative state).

A meditator: One should keep faith in the Creator and not think too much.

Billu: Yes and no, both. Ignorance is generally a curse but can be very blissful at times. Hindus are not fortunately forbidden from thinking and asking questions. The current legal and justice systems in the world are based mainly on the thinking of such great thinkers as Aristotle, Socrates, Plato and other great philosophers. The basic principle of evolution, as Mother Nature has designed us, is 'we lose what we don't use'!

Regular meditation is a must but regular *karma* (conscientious action) must also follow it.

Subash: Yes, yes...Regular Meditation followed by regular activity as per individual requirements is important. Thinking also is equally necessary. Maharishi used to say, 'One who can think can also Meditate.' Those who have no thinking power cannot be as expressive. So we should think as big as we can; it is a necessary part of the human evolution and hence overall development.

### Republic Day Jan 2016

Billu: Greetings on India's Republic Day. This day is also celebrated in Australia as the Australia Day. As a true son of the soil, I am required to be a good ambassador for both my countries—India and Australia and help to stitch the two countries together. Active citizenship always, whether I am in India or in Australia, is my expectation from myself. My life and service is for both my countries.

Subash: Any good and conscious person feels as if he belongs to the whole world and not only countries that he is directly concerned with. *Vasudhaiva Kutumbakam* (the world is one family of the Lord).

Billu: Australia is home to people who were born overseas in nearly 160 countries, so it is a smaller scale of the world.

God loves and gives to all but our own (cumulative) karma comes in-between. A tree does not stop bad people from plucking its fruits or flowers. Sun does not stop shining on bad people. Air too does not discriminate and neither does Mother Earth!

Our *karma* makes our destiny. So long as we stay closer to our conscience and constantly listen to it, and don't do any *adharmic* (means 'immoral') activity, we remain good. When we stop listening to our Conscience, it also stops guiding us. And that marks the beginning of *adharmic* activities and our future sufferings.

Subash: That is how it works...Those who are consciously awake feel God's presence always, while it is *vice versa* for the other category...the reality that we could talk about should be self-referral. *Vaishnav Jantu te niz kahiye jo Peed parayi Jaaney re* (non-violent persons harbour compassion and empathy for other people and suffer with all those who are in pain)...it can be possible only when it is self-referral.

Jyotsna Jotshi: While having my medicine in the morning, I suddenly remembered something. Thought of sharing it. One night, I was giving Bhaisahib his medicines and when he put them in his mouth, I realised that I had forgotten to bring water along. I rushed down to the kitchen and brought a glass of water as fast as I could. After having the water, Bhaisahib asked me why I panicked. I told him how bad I felt that he had to keep those bitter pills in his mouth for such a long time. He smiled and said, 'It is just a type of taste. You will face lots of bitter tastes in life and you will have two choices...to panic or be calm. Panic will lead to chaos and so on but waiting for water to remove the bitterness will not only remove the distaste but also show how wise and composed you are'.

Billu: Human fears, both known and unknown are at the root of endless human worries, anxieties, miseries etc. For reasonable and 'known' fears, we generally put prudent management measures in place. But, for dealing with 'unknown, imaginary' fears, we tend to overuse our brain and suffer from unnecessary and undue mental stress. This is where the advice is intended to help us.

> *O bird of the morning, learn love from the moth;*
> *Because it burnt, lost its life, found no voice;*
> *These pretenders are ignorant in search of Him;*
> *Because he who obtained knowledge has not returned*
> —Sa'di, the Persian poet

Sa'di Shirazi (1210-1292) was a great Persian writer-philosopher (mystic) who penned his writings in the form of beautiful poems. Amongst his great works, *Bustan* and *Gulistan* (garden of flowers) stand out. At the entrance hall of the UN office in the US, alongside a very large Persian carpet, Sa'di's words dazzle:

> *All human beings are members of one frame,*
> *Since all, at first, from the same essence came.*
> *When time afflicts a limb with pain*
> *The other limb at rest cannot remain.*
> *If thou feel not for other's misery*
> *A human being is no name for thee.*

In one of his stories, he is supposed to have said:

*Do not order pounded meat for my table. To a pounded man, simple bread is pounded meat. The thirsty look in their sleep on the whole world as a spring of water.*

Like Saadi, Rumi (1207-1273) was also a great Persian mystic, philosopher and poet. He said: 'Let the beauty we love be what we do. There are hundreds of ways to kneel and kiss the ground. What you seek is seeking you. Be like melting snow, wash yourself of yourself. Why do you stay in prison when the door is wide open. Out beyond ideas of right-doing and wrongdoing, there is a field. I will meet you there. And you? When will you begin that long journey into yourself. Stop acting so small. You are the universe in ecstatic motion. The wound is the place where the Light enters you. When you do things from your soul, you feel a river moving in you, a joy.'

### Simplicity Feb 2016

It is generally believed that people do what they have always done and how they have always done things. Old habits die very hard and unlearning is impossible with most. As a result, some people can never keep it simple.

One of the migrant Kashmiri aunties from India, in her late seventies (a medical doctor by profession) had been very keen to cook *subz hakh* (green kailan) the way Kashmiris cook. She repeatedly asked Rekha how it looks, what is it called in the local vegetable shops (*kailan* is the Chinese name) and how do we cook it? One day she excitedly called Rekha and said that she had cooked it. Guess how she had done it! She had cooked it the way she cooks most other things, but a little differently. She had boiled it first and then cooked it with onion, garlic and tomato. She just could not believe and adopt the simple way in which Kashmiris cook their *subz hakh*!

The above real life story has a direct correlation with many things that we do, including TM. Some people just can't keep things simple and don't stick to the basics. Likewise, experiencing God is also not that difficult if…

Subash: *Kaash yeh if naa hota toh Billuji…yeh jagat hi shayad nahi hota* (if it was not such, this world would not have existed).

### The Exodus of Kashmiri Pandits Feb 2016

Billu: On 5 Jan 2016, after the recent Pathankot episode, I wrote the following painful email to one of our very close friends, an ex IAF decorated pilot (Mahavir Chakra Vijeta, 1971). He is still very fit and trains foreign pilots on behalf of the Royal Australian Air Force (RAAF):

I respect your faith in Indian government's ability to deal with this unfortunate situation and your optimism that they will finally prevail over the enemy. I hope time proves you right! My grief and personal views (with doubt/frustration) on the situation are shaped by my personal trauma (pre-1990) and suffering (post-1990) as a result of a combination of factors, including (a) the devious role of Pakistan and shocking betrayal by our Muslim fraternity; (b) the then Indian government's inability to save our life and honour and prevent our mass exodus from our homeland; and (c) obvious indifference and lack of compassion/apathy/ignorance shown towards us KPs by the millions of so called pseudo-secular/educated Hindus. Please read that book (by Rahul Pandita) to have a peep into the hell that we have lived.

Last week, the visiting father (in early 70s) of a social contact from Delhi seemed to be very critical of PM Modi, instead he was praising Kejriwal like anything (because of reduced water bills). He did not know much about the exodus of KPs in 1990. Adding salt to my wounds, he asked me, '*phir woh 5 lakh pandit kahan gaye*? (then where did those five lakh Pandits go?)'

Earlier, during our life in Malaysia in the mid-nineties, I was shocked to find that none of our ten Indian expatriate friends had any clue about the exodus of KPs from the valley.

One important question arises: 'Why did (do) we KPs not matter to the Indian media and the diaspora? Why are we so insignificant? Because we are not a menace to anyone or because we don't form a major vote bank?'

*Australia and Australians Feb 2016*
Billu: The commonly used hearing device (bionic ear) and Penicillin were developed by Australians—Graeme Clark and Alexander Fleming, respectively. Perth Professor, Barry Marshal, received Nobel Prize in medicine a few years ago. Perth Professor Fiona Wood is a revolutionary burn specialist.

Most educated Aussies believe themselves to be world citizens. Their thinking is reflected in their actions across the globe—unconditional, open-hearted donations, physical relief, volunteering in assistance during natural disasters, etc.

In comparison to others, Aussies are relatively humble and modest, although they punch much above their weight. God bless this country! On any day, I feel very humbled to see how people here work and think. No one claims to be religious or spiritual. They don't even know much about spirituality but their thoughts and actions reflect spirituality of a high order, always in action.

About 70 per cent Aussies don't practice any religion! You may call them atheists, if you choose. However, in my view, their thoughts and actions are very spiritual without them even knowing about it. They don't care about it but do care about the world!

People have a high sense of materialistic detachment; they try to live in the moment. This country does not encourage one's personal ego. The great Mirza Ghalib wrote:

*Na tha kuch to, Khuda tha, Aur na kuch hoga, Khuda hoga.*
*Mitaya muj ko hone ne na hota main to kya hota.*

In that beautiful couplet, Ghalib defined the concept of the cosmos, time, God and the human existence—physical and spiritual, with strong relevance to human ego. Ghalib also seems to hint towards the concept of *sifar* (*shunya*, zero) and its relevance in our spiritual journey, like the great Kashmiri poetess, Lal Ded!

There is something in this ancient spiritual land of Indigenous Aboriginal Australians! This country forces one to think critically and outside the box.

Subash: Yes...their such great qualities allow them to search for newer and newer horizons... because they are highly spirited and spirit (Natural Quality) does not belong to any specific religion...it is the reality and such nice human beings are so flexible with a higher sense of adaptability and that is why Maharishi could spread TM around the globe more speedily...They are nature lovers and hence natural...not selfish but carefree...and hence lead the way to newer and newer achievements and greater heights... When the number of such spirited human beings rise...the possibility of the Heaven on Earth will become more visible.

### *Power of Selfless Love Feb 2016*
Billu: That reminds me of a story about a rampaging elephant who bowed at the feet of Gautam Buddha. Everyone, except the Buddha, was frightened and ran away on seeing the elephant running towards them. Again, as always, the onus is well and truly on us.

I watched a documentary, *Inshallah Kashmir*, where Khemlata Wakhlu and Professor O N Wakhlu (my esteemed teacher) were also interviewed. They spent about six months or more in the captivity of Kashmiri militants in the early nineties. Their fate changed (for the good) when one day Mrs Wakhlu slapped a young militant for smoking. She said her 'fearless action' was borne out of her motherly love (and care) towards the young militant and her concern for his health. They said the whole attitude of all the nine militants changed suddenly after that incident.

### *God & Spirituality Feb 2016*
Billu: There is a difference between dreams and reality. In dreams, God exists outside of us, but in reality, God dwells in each one of us! First we must love ourselves, ie. who we truly are, and then see ourselves present in every life form out there—human, bird or animal. Once that happens, we truly experience that pure love from within our bosom for the world outside. Then magic happens!

O P Kakroo: Advent of positive forces compels churning in the society. Positive and negative forces get clearly demarcated and separated like before *ksheer sagar manthan* or Mahabharata.

Similar is happening in India and at the world level. Shall we be witness to a New Mahabharata?

Vinod: Thought is powerful and emanates from the mind; collective thought becomes a force in geometric progression if conjoined with physical contact. If it remains aloof, it has the effect of arithmetic progression.

O P Kakroo: A meditator's thought is always coherent and collective irrespective of physical contact, being connected to a common field as told by Maharishi.

Billu: TM provides depth to the human intellect and growth to the wisdom. The mind becomes settled and clear, and flows calmly but with enormous strength, just like a deep river. With that depth and clarity in mind, it is relatively much easier to address and tackle serious issues.

In our journey, we have tried to apprise scores of educated, prominent Pakistanis about what really happened in the valley and who are the real victim there, which was to their absolute surprise and utter shock. By their humble admission and deep regret, Pakistanis have been misled by their *mullahs*, based on what some Kashmiris have been feeding them.

With a sustained and sincere dialogue, over time, these Pakistanis have become our friends. Otherwise, could you imagine, for the last 10 years or more immediately after their Id prayers, a group of around 15 to 20 people (4 to 5 families) visit us and seek the blessings of my father, as a revered *buzarg* (an elder) when he is here in Perth, and have breakfast at our home? Over time, these Pakistanis must have conveyed the reality to thousands back home. In the end, hostility should reduce to some extent. If one family could do it, imagine what 10,000 families can do and so on!

Vinod: A meditator means a person with expanded awareness and infinite alertness, in perfection and unison with the source of creativity.

It is not being fearless, it is reporting things as they are and presenting mirror image without refraction, deviation and deflection, but being purely incidental and reflecting purity without concealing parts or full, out of fear.

If we don't speak of things as they are, we are concealing and playing deception, which can give time for consolidation to the person who has a problematic mentality. We have have to be fearless and say things as they are.

### Kashmiri Pandits & Vote Bank Feb 2016

Billu: Vote bank and political menace! This is what gives any community importance in a political scenario. Unfortunately, KPs don't have any. KPs don't contribute effectively to anyone's vote bank. So, it is no surprise that not many people in India find KPs interesting and important. Practically, we are just numbers. Plus, the way we have been relatively spending money lavishly in public, for example, in the manner we perform our wedding ceremonies, has not earned us many sympathisers in the Indian diaspora.

KPs have always leaned on themselves to survive. Individually, KPs outperform most other people from other communities, but only by dint of their literacy, intelligence and hard work. *Khuda he hafiz hai hum batoon ka* (God is our sole saviour). As the Biblical saying goes, 'God helps those who help themselves!', This advice is absolutely valid and applicable to us KPs.

Interestingly, we KPs don't even have one view or one voice or one action plan *vis-a-vis* our forced exodus from the Valley. Can you imagine, what an elderly KP father said in a public forum about our exodus? He said, 'KPs have used exodus as an '"excuse" for leaving Kashmir. They have benefitted from the exodus and prospered only after their migration. They wouldn't even "get a seat" in Kashmir (medical/engineering).'

Currently, in my honest opinion, the need of the hour is to undertake the following two-pronged action plan:

(a) Social engineering—that is to rediscover who we KPs truly are, what defines us, what are our values, and how will we survive as one KP community? *Naam ke KP or asli KP?* (KPs in name only or the real KPs?); and

(b) Reclaim our nursing/breeding ground—that is to 'help ourselves' to find a niche back in the valley. No one will help us because neither do we form the vote bank nor are we a menace to anyone. We have to make bridges ourselves, as always. We left the valley of our own volition and Jagmohan or India did not pull us out, as claimed by the people living across the Banihal ranges.

For a community to survive, in addition to their spirituality and the thought, two things are most important—food and language. If these change, the community changes! Currently, we are under a serious direct threat on both these fronts. Remember that 'literacy' and 'education' are two different things.

A person can be called a literate, but may practically be uneducated. Our ancestors were by and large educated, even though some may have been illiterate.

A Meditator: Respected Koul sahib, food and language will survive only when we have our homeland. For the survival of language, marriages within the community is important. Let us educate our children of the benefits of marrying within the community.

Billu: Not as individuals, but as a community. Can we lead the world, as an example? It is important that we remain KPs, in both deed and thought, and not transform into something else. These are various challenges that we need to overcome in order to regain our character and *the* core values. All these tasks are possible if we are stable within, so we should take care of our physical fitness and spiritual and mental health.

O P Kakroo: *Ku Budhi ka Naash aur Satbudhi ka Prakash* (God, replace the evil thoughts with noble thoughts).

Billu: Nationalism and patriotism of KPs (as a community) is without a match. We have paid a huge price for it in 1989-1990 and during the following years. My personal guesstimate based on my interaction across the planet Earth, is that less than 20% Indians are really aware about our painful and tragic history and our direct physical and mental suffering due to our exodus. That is a reality. If lucky, we may be able to change it to some extent only by dialogue and education of our fellow Indians.

*Himmeteh marda, muddeh Khuda* (God helps those who help themselves), wrote the great poet Iqbal, who also wrote, *Saare Jahan se acha Hindustan humara....* He also wrote, *Khudee ko bhuland kar itna....*

### Downside of Caste System Feb 2016

Rohit: (Forwards a post about the Brahmins and their demographic information.) A study team of Brahmins worked for two months on the status of Brahmins in all states and prepared a brief note on the study. The Brahmins should know their position and power in the country.

Billu: The statistical, demographical data about Brahmins may be very inspiring for Brahmins but it has the potential to be extremely discouraging and alarming for the persons belonging to the other castes.

It does not matter whether the data is authentic or forged, it will help to divide the Indian community, one way or the other. It is quite possible that this popular social media post may have been the work of a non-Brahmin, with an intention to raise an alarm with people belonging to other castes.

Long back, when I was studying at the University of Roorkee, I experienced how people treated me differently based on my caste. In the beginning, when we were new to the town, most people would ask me about my caste, some thought I was *Angrez* (a white man) and would speak with me only in English. Initially, I was naive and would tell them readily that I was a Kashmiri Pandit. I observed that some people would then treat me with respect whereas some people would frown. Later on, on somebody's good advice, I would only tell them that I was a Hindu, without divulging my caste, and that helped. Same thing has happened recently in Haryana; people had to hide their surnames to protect themselves.

It is time that we transcend these man-made divisions and recognise ourselves as humans only. Why do we need a stamp on our forehead? What changes? From Kashmir, we were driven out by our Muslim brethren. In Roorkee, our Dhobi/press-wala (a person who irons clothes) did not give us his first bill for about three months, he just did not have the courage! Why? He kept on saying, very humbly, *jo aapki marzi* (as you wish to), when we would ask for his bill. Hey Ram! We had to do the maths to pay him after about 3 months—5 clothes on average for 90 days, 25 paisa each (1986) + 10 per cent. Where is the fairness?

### An Academic Political Activist Feb 2016

A Meditator: People like her (an academic political activist) should read the history of concentration camps in all so called communist countries crying hoarse for social parity. Does she really have a soul?

Billu: Definitely yes, all such people have souls, covered under thick layers of lust and corruption. Even butchers have souls! Our daily bath cleans out bodies. Our daily TM cleans our conscience. These people need TM.

Another Meditator: Yes indeed, they need to taste the nectar of meditation.

Billu: Bhaisahib had initiated a number of Arab and Palestinian students (in Kashmir) into TM without converting them. That tells you what spirituality means.

If you still call yourself a Hindu and say Hinduism is the best religion of all, you place yourself within human boundaries and, thus, are separating yourself from the rest of the world.

O P Kakroo: With your permission, just an intervention! Who wants liberation? I don't! We just want to do TM and enjoy your company.

Billu: Those words of wisdom can only ooze from a liberated mind as yours. Pardon my audacity. With my seemingly annoying and provocative attitude, not many people find me likeable. I am overwhelmed by your love.

Subash: *Doori Mitaye.....Bharat aajaye......Prakash fyalaayey* (Cover the distance and return to India and spread light).

### Slope Failure & Mental Sickness March 2016

Billu: I am currently looking at the aerial photograph of the Mata Vaishno Devi Shrine. It seems a major drainage channel is passing right through the area where the slope failure has occurred.

I am alarmed to see people perched (on the left side of the photo) right over an area which is heavily undermined. The authorities must immediately evacuate the local area within a radius of at least 50 m from the failure, till things are fixed and alternate safe pedestrian paths are identified and prepared.

If natural waterways and drainage channels are blocked, this is what happens. Water must always be given passage to move unhindered due to natural gravity.

I hope the authorities consult a qualified and seasoned geotechnical engineer to address this matter ASAP.

There is the potential for all structures sitting above the slope failure to collapse as well, if the drainage line is blocked and if the subsoil has already experienced some movement. It is a matter of time.

Does anyone know anyone from the Shrine Board? If yes, please request him to immediately clear the area of people, as suggested above, and bring an experienced team of geotechnical engineers to assess the situation at the site and map the whole area. This is not a job for a general civil engineer. It needs specialists.

Soils and rocks comprise solid particles and pore spaces between those particles. These pore spaces can be dry or wet or partly wet in different situations, which controls the behaviour of the soil mass. Sandy soils allow relatively free flow of water. However, clayey soils are relatively far less permeable.

In natural slopes (hills) and manmade slopes (dams, embankments), for slope stability, it is essential that groundwater, surface water is provided with a path to flow freely, without causing any ponding within the soil mass behind the surface of the slope. Ponding of water causes excessive hydrostatic pressure behind the slope surface which adds to the gravitational destabilising forces. In hilly areas, random, poorly planned, manmade structures have the potential to obstruct the natural waterways (during rainfall events), triggering off landslides. Forces due to friction between particles resist the destabilising forces. Natural vegetation, roots bind the soil mass similar to steel reinforcement.

In short, if water is not allowed to flow naturally, problems occur due to build-up of excessive hydrostatic pressure, which can transform into hydrodynamic forces. Similarly, if the human mind is not provided with a mechanism to release mental pressure, stress, problems do occur.

*Kath-bath* (chi-chat) is extremely important for mental health. Thanks to our gurus for TM and our Dear Kakroo sahib for creating this beautiful forum where we share our thoughts and feelings. In the western world, there is a golden rule—no question is stupid. Therefore, please use this forum usefully and with purpose to vent your thoughts, regardless of any inhibition. All learn.

Do you know why rivers flowing through mountains gorges (eg.*Chinab*) appear to be so silent (*shaant*) although they flow considerably much faster than when flowing through plains. The answer is: they flow much deeper within the mountain gorges.

Why do rivers need to flow deeper in mountain gorges? The answer is, 'Deep rivers are bound on both sides by strong and massive rock mass which does not yield much, so they have no other way to contain their water (discharge) other than to deepen to increase their capacity (volume).'

Rakesh Safaya: *Aap apni life aur TM ke upar koi kitab kyun nahi likhte... Aap bada achcha likhte ho...* (why don't you write a book on your life and the TM; you write well). Writing a book is the right thing to express yourself. What were the changes in your life after learning TM and what does TM mean to you?

Billu: After work, at the end of the day, when I get a little time, all I want to do is to be with myself, so how can I write a book? When I think of writing a book, my mind goes blank. I write generally during work, immediately after my morning run. TM has created spontaneity in my actions. A day has only 24 hours. As long as you people will listen to what I am saying, I'll keep writing.

### Faith May 2016

Bhaisahib would tell a mythological story of *Brahmarishi Narad Muni* and his conversation with two sadhus. One was meditating under a very large tree and the other under a much smaller tree.

The sage sitting under the smaller tree asked the *Narad Muni* how many years he would take to meet *Narayan*. To which, *Narad Muni* replied, 'as many as the number of leaves on the tree under which you are sitting.' The sage became very sad and said, 'Oh, so many?' He stood up and walked away.

After a while, at a different location, *Narad Muni* met another sage who was sitting under a much larger tree. He asked *Narad* the same question and *Narad* replied likewise. On hearing this, the sage beamed with great joy and exclaimed with excitement, 'So, after all those years, I'll be definitely meeting *Narayan*. Great, no problems!' He bowed respectfully to *Narad* and continued his meditation cheerfully. On hearing this, *Narad* said,'Oh sage, seeing your faith and determination, you will possibly take very less time to meet *Narayan*; you are very close, or perhaps you may already be there with Him.'

### Stick to the Constant and not the Variable June 2016

Would we be different (with different thoughts) if we were born in a different religion or a different country? Most of us may say 'yes'. The question then arises why and what part of us would have been different? Given that the Truth is constant, why would we vary? The vital question finally arises—which part of us is Constant and which part varies?

Answer to the above question leads us to a practical challenge, ie. what do we do to remain constant (if that is a priority) and not be defined as a variable? As a clue, if we are asked, 'Who are you?', how many of us would answer, 'I am a human being', instead of 'I am a man, I am a Hindu, I am a Kashmiri Pandit or I am an Indian?'

O P Kakroo: If consciousness is not evolving, then one is not doing the right kind of meditation.

Billu: One day, I asked Bhaisahib about a certain gentleman, who was also a meditator. In my opinion, that person was a bit complicated and unpredictable. Bhaisahib said, 'Meditation can't turn a crow into a white swan. A crow will not stop nibbling, but the intensity of its nibble will mellow'.

Acceptance is the key to happiness (or actually the absence of unhappiness), but it is not that easy. One has to be blessed.

Human mind plays tricks and games. It is very fickle. Meditation and *Guru Kripa* are the only tools that help to stabilise it to an extent where it can 'accept' the things and start witnessing rather than getting involved.

### Vandalism of a Hindu temple in Jammu June 2016

Ravi Bharti: As per the reports, today at around 18:45, one Mohd Yaseer vandalised the Aap Shambu Temple. Later, he was arrested by the Flying Squad of Janipur Police Station. As the news spread, the local people have started protests and blocked the road opposite the police station. Protests in the area are going on and a mob of around 1000 people is reported to have gathered; the situation appears to be volatile.

Bill Koul: An absolutely disgusting act! He is mentally deranged. Such elements are extremely inflammable and, therefore, must be lodged in a maximum security prison. I hope the *Dharamarth Trust* imparts adequate self-defence training to all priests and caretakers. This person should have been physically overpowered and immobilised in the very early moments of his rampage.

I would have been equally disgusted if a Hindu would have carried out such a disgusting act in a church or a mosque. Such acts cause pain to the believers, regardless of their faith. They are also humans. Everyone's belief must be respected.

As an old trick, this horrible and horrendous act seems to have been staged deliberately to stir up the Hindu-Muslim issue during the current Ramadan days. I hope the Jammu people remain restrained. There are thousands of Hindus currently in Kashmir who may be targeted.

Restraint and immunity are required. As we immunise ourselves from the diseases, we must immunise our community.

Some mischievous elements want Hindus to be violent which will help to convert their moderates into fundamentals.

Blood wants blood. They want to spill blood. It does not matter how many people die on either side, the tragedy is that all who die will be humans—sons, brothers, fathers. The world is fighting this menace and struggling to control it.

Lord Shiva does not need protection from us humans.

Hindus must not fall in the trap. It is a trap. All cool heads on either side must work together to prevent any bloodshed. Hindus must become strong enough, not for attacking and killing, but for showing a strong defence. It should work like the immunisation of a human body. The body must become strong to resist the infection; the virus is everywhere around it; it can't be seen with the naked eye. We don't go after the virus, we focus on strengthening ourselves.

Again, the temple caretakers should be imparted the necessary training to defend themselves and the temple property and control such nuisance well in time.

Ravi Bharti: Yes Sir, you have rightly hit the nail on the head. But, where are the Hindus? We are either Brahmins, Baniyas, Khatris or from so-called lower castes. As for strengthening, lesser said the better. Yes, we want to strengthen groups based on locations, castes, sub-castes and language etc.

Our caste system has created tall silos and cracks within the people of India, which potentially weaken the defence system.

Billu: Now that the problem has been illustrated, what is the solution? Who amongst us will play a part in the solution? As no one amongst us will be prepared to bell the cat, it is just a time wasting activity to keep discussing the problem. We should do only what we are trained to do: Meditate. Leave the problem to the people whom you vote to form the government and have faith in God as we have been groomed to do since our birth. If anyone has any meaningful solution and an action plan, take the lead.

## Gender Bias July 2016

I would like your advice on my query as to why is the Supreme Being a 'He' and why is God a 'He'? We are all born from our mothers, who practically represent our first Gods. As for the Creation, we thought it was the Mother Nature. Don't you think that by terming the God as 'He', we are no different to others? A simple explanation will do.

Most religious texts of other religions keep the man at a higher pedestal than a woman. However, in practical terms, a woman is much more powerful and creative than a man. Genetically, she is also stronger. Shouldn't, therefore, God be a 'She'?

K L Munshi: If Shiva is Light, Shakti is its dispersion. We are all *sat chit ananda* in essence, beyond pairs of opposites... neither male nor female.

Ravinder K Raina: Well said, Dr Munshi, beautifully analysed. Moreover, we do not have the time and interest to compare with the other religions. Time is running out. Just meditate and get the answers. There are lots of things unrevealed. Just meditate to be the best.

Billu: In the simple terms, would you agree with me that God is neither a He nor She? On a different subject, if spirituality could be inculcated by religious texts and the intellect, this world would have been different! Unlearning is important to let go of our shackles. Trotkachrya is a fine example. Bhakti and love, for one and all, are what matter in spirituality!

K L Munshi: Love, joy, peace, beauty cannot be measured.

Billu: I have only been trying to put across a different perspective. I am sick of our societies being male-centric. We men have empowered ourselves much disproportionately, which is not much dissimilar to the people of other faiths. Please pardon me if I have trespassed.

Subhash: Any or all societies comprise of Individuals and the amalgamation of Individual thoughts, views and ways of life form the socio-cultural fabric of such societies. I can't think of any TM meditator who can be gripped by the gender bias. As Dr Munshi sahib has illustrated in his post above, Shiv and Shakti are one and the same at a particular level of higher consciousness. One beholds the other and at the higher levels of consciousness, our seers have mentioned both as one. Singularity is just one and in layman's language, we can also say worship Mata and you'll find Shiva and same is true as *vice versa*. Get hold of one and you will find both.

Billu: Unnecessary to prolong this discussion; there is nothing new which you people are saying and which we did not already know as grownups.

One last time, my simple question was: Why do we commonly address God as 'He'? This question has practical relevance for our young children.

I think I owe you all the simpler answer to my question. It is:

This is how we (me included) have been brought up and trained by our elders since we started listening and speaking. Our spiritual awakening has not caused a practical transformation.

Rekha: Interesting conversations around the equity of diverse groups since yesterday!

Thanks Billuji, for at least acknowledging the gender gap. Both you and I have a long way to go before the balance is restored. The simplest example is my role as a mother. At times, I also undo this balance by an unconscious bias, which could be the resultant of my learnt behaviours. Your thoughts are encouraging for women in our society, which hopefully may start a positive change.

Universal philosophy has never been discriminatory, but the questions are: Is it really being practised or are the members of the society (both males and females) even aware about this gap? If yes, how many of us are ready to work towards bridging this gap?

The answers to all these questions are not in the religious philosophy but in our everyday life philosophy, which can be transformative.

Let us march towards the right direction to restore the much desired gender balance.

## A KASHMIRI PANDIT GROUP IN PERTH

A social media chatting forum, called '*Batta Boys of Perth*' has been created by relatively younger Pandit boys about three years ago.

The group comprises around 25 male members. Most of the members have technical qualifications.

The following chats provide a significant snapshot of the current mindset of young Kashmiri Pandit youth, their interests and aspirations.

On the basis of these chats, several important questions arise: How different are these chats from the conversations of traditional Kashmiri Pandit men in terms of the nature of the topics discussed therein and the quality of the language used by the chatters, i.e. would our ancestors also have used the same or similar language? To what extent do our relatively younger men represent the traditional Pandit thought, language and the general mindset, i.e. how much Kashmiri are our youth at present, in terms of their culture? Pursuant to the aforementioned second question, if any change has occurred in our younger generation over time, if and to what extent has the exodus of Pandits from Kashmir been responsible for the change? As the younger generation, especially those currently in their thirties, will predominantly drive the traditional Kashmiri culture in the next thirty years, how much Kashmiri would our future generations be?

It is generally believed that food and language play a significant role in keeping the culture of an ethnic group alive.

Given that most Kashmiri Pandits generally speak in English and/or *Hindustani* (ie. mixture of Hindi and Urdu) at home, with only a few or no words of Kashmiri, it may be a matter of only a few decades that Kashmiri language may potentially become extinct amongst Pandits living outside Kashmir. Will our so called Kashmiri food, such as *roganjosh* or *dum alloo*, be deemed to be sufficient to keep our Kashmiri culture alive, as some people believe at present? Importantly, will these dishes be left unchanged? It is not uncommon to see some people on the internet, restaurants/hotels and non-Kashmiris and even some Kashmiris, cooking *dum alloos* using tomato and onion. Same goes for *roganjosh*. Traditionally, tomato and onion is not used in cooking both these Kashmiri dishes. So, there is already a significant shift occurring in the cooking of our traditional signature cuisine. The most important question of all: Is the Pandit community facing a clear and present danger that our future generation will remain Kashmiri only in their name? If yes, what are we doing about that?

Unfortunately, the scenario is not much different in the valley itself, where families and children, especially from the elite, educated and professional class, communicate mainly in Urdu and English. Therefore, return to the valley may not be an effective solution.

It seems, most educated, professional and elite Kashmiris, irrespective of the religious divide, have consciously been choosing a non-Kashmiri language as their preferred language at home and outside their home.

As a broader Kashmiri community, what are the reasons that we feel inferior to the others? Why don't we take pride in being a Kashmiri? What conscious and deliberate steps must the whole Kashmiri community take as a matter of urgency?

Before the above questions are answered, the big question is: Does the Kashmiri community, comprising both Muslims and Pandits, recognise that we Kashmiris are potentially facing the possibility of our ethnic extinction?

### Naga & the Attire of Kashmiri Women April 2016

Mythologically Kashmir valley was inhabited by the *Nagas* (a species of serpents who could, at will, transform into humans and back) before and at the time of her settlement by *Kashyap Rishi*. Kashmiri folk tales provide a good insight into their lives. Sightings of *Nagas* have continued to be reported by people living away from the Srinagar city.

The traditional dress of Kashmiri women is *Phirun*, with head gear comprising *kalpush, zooj, taranga, poochh* and *deaj*.

The *Poochh* is connected with a muslin piece of white cloth, about 4 feet long (down to ankles), hanging at the back. The entire head gear and the hanging tail depict the shale of a *naga*. The head gear depicts the hood and the pooch tail depicts the body of the snake *(naga)*.

We must respect our women. They represent our mothers, sisters and daughters. We would not have existed without them and the blessings of Mother Nature in both her natural and human forms.

### Kashmiri Pandit Role Models April 2016

How often do we discipline and scold our children when they say and do certain (wrong) things? And how often do we find ourselves saying and doing the same very things, or even worse, at times?

TVS: To lead by example and practicing what one preaches is an essential mantra in life. We young parents would certainly value your thoughts. Especially raising the next generation (our first) outside home. Hard to do without experience and guidance from elders of our community! Any thoughts from young guns? How has it been growing up here? Anything to watch out for?

KZS: Very true! We as human beings are creatures of self-interest. For 90% of us, our thoughts, ideology, principles and judgement changes to suit our interests at that moment, sometimes even involuntarily. We preach to others not to do what we ourselves have done at some point in time. It is important to refrain from such hypocritical behaviour, with our children or anyone else, for it causes loss of respect and acrimony in relations

Billu: I am not very sure about myself—if I have been a good role model or not for our children. The family mantra has been: 'Keep it simple stupid (kiss)', which is in line with my approach in the professional world.

My world and my greater family extend much beyond my home and my immediate family. I care for all and try to assist others to the extent possible; however, I have burnt my fingers on numerous occasions. Having said that, my basic helping nature has not changed, however, my approach has indeed changed.

### What does Bhatta mean? May 2016

Billu: The word *bhatta* is a distorted version of the Sanskrit word *bhatt*, which means the 'learned one'. In Jammu, however, the meaning of the word '*bhatt*' is altogether different (where it means a stone).

In the seventies and eighties, during my growing up years in Kashmir, Pandits would be distinctly identified by their cleaner appearance, higher education on average, high intelligence and a civil/clean spoken language. By the late eighties, however, the average Kashmiri Muslims, in particular, the educated and professionals and the Muslims of the upper socio-economic class had remarkably overtaken the average Pandits in terms of sophistication and the polish in their spoken language. Even the boatmen (*hanjis*) had remarkably strived and achieved some degree of sophistication.

Our public behaviour, appearance, food preferences, habits and the language, both written and spoken, in both formal and informal settings, define us. What we write on any forum, more often than not, passes through the eyes of our life partners and children, in particular our daughters. Therefore, to prevent potential loss of face and respect and possible embarrassment, extreme care is requested (rather begged) while writing our posts.

It would be useful also to read Professor Somnath Wakhlu's book, *Kashmiri Pandit-Cultural & Historical Introduction*, for rediscovering who we are supposed to be.

### *A mini-Israel for Pandits May 2016*
BXR: (Forwards a picture of Srinagar)

Billu: Thanks for that beautiful picture of Srinagar, showing those *doongas* (houseboats) in the *Vitastaa* (River Jhelum); and Hari Parbat in the background. The bridge may be either the 5th or the 6th bridge.

TXS: Really a serene view! Hope we all go together and visit Kashmir (can be only as a tourist).

BXR: It must be past Nowhatta. Can do for sure...am planning to go there these holidays. Air Asia direct to Delhi cheap flights!

I had a good time; of course the people there treat you like visitors. Does every KP support a separate composite township in Kashmir for KPs? Now there is a very serious effort by the Indian Central Govt for the same. There is also a Kashmiri Muslim group which is supporting this idea of KPs to have a separate township for them. Those Kashmiri Muslims, comprising doctors, engineers, academicians etc. are active on social networking and condemn those Kashmiri leaders who oppose the idea of a separate township for the KPs.

ZXA: I support separate suburbs (secured obviously) for KPs within Srinagar to start with and then eventually if the situation ever gets safer for KPs in general, then our community can move out to other suburbs within Srinagar and the Kashmir valley. We need an anchor in Srinagar/Kashmir.

BXR: That is exactly what this new Kashmiri Muslim support group is propagating. They have even gone to an extent of condemning Kashmiri leaders for creating a rift between the two communities in Kashmir.

ZXA: We should learn from the Jews. Even when their population was in millions, they were pioneers in all fields (engineering, banking, arts and everything you name it). They still are. They were treated like shit by other people for 2,000 years since they were kicked out of Israel. After they were almost terminated by Hitler and other Christians in Europe, they fought/lobbied for their homeland in present day Israel and won it. We all know how powerful Israel is now. We need a mini Israel for KPs within Kashmir.

Jews were scattered all over the world and had no country to call their homeland. That is why they were always kicked around. Once they got their homeland in present day Israel, no one messes with them.

KYB: Problem with Battas is we have a country but no land.

BXR: Jews claimed their homeland after thousands of years. And we have the land, the government in Centre to support.

KYB: Where is the land? In Kashmir?

BXR: All we need is to create KP groups all around world to get attention to our cause; the whole of Kashmir is our land.

KYB: Will Kashmiri Battas invest in the land and pack their bags to go back? Unlike the Jews, the Battas are with homes. How many would want to uproot themselves and move to a hostile environment. A simple question to you first; will you move back?

BXR: What do you think? Will you go?

KYB: I am asking you.

BXR: Same question can be asked to you as well.

KYB: And how many will be willing to go. If you insist on me answering first, I will not.

BXR: I respect your decision.

KYB: Thank you. You didn't answer.

BXR: I will act when time comes but I am willing to go back.

KYB: Retirement is not the time to go back. If settlement of land is required, younger generation has to move back and toil the land in the sun, which none of us has done ever. So easier said than done!

ZXA: There are lot of Battas in Jammu who are more than happy to go back to Kashmir. Also, with free (or let's say cheap) land, Batta will go anywhere.

KYB: And then sell it and make hay elsewhere. Is that what we want?

ZXA: There will be such people who will like to do exactly what you said. But once they see that the community in general wants to stay and live there, maybe they will change. Very few Jews wanted to go back to Israel when it was made, as they were afraid of the unknown and it was not easy for them either. Soon Israel became a country. All of the Muslim world and most of the European countries went against them. Our own M K Gandhi went against Israel. Surrounding Arab nations invaded Israel a couple of times but against all odds it won.

BXR: ... summarised it all. Not all Jews live in Israel but their heart and soul is for Israel.

ZXA: Yes. They send lots of funds to Israel and work to influence western governments like the US, EU and Australia. We can learn a lot from them.

BXR: The economic disparity all around the world is getting narrow and if same conditions are created in Kashmir, who knows even younger generation may want to go back as well.

PXA: Gents, I don't blame Hurriyat or Muslims...The problems lies in Battas within...We can't be united....In the last 50 years we haven't been able to nominate one leader...There are more than 100 Kashmiri Pandit parties and everyone has their own manifesto...Look at the Muslims....How united are they globally? Forget the Pandits, look at the Hindus, or the Sikh community?

BXR: KPs always try to project themselves as apolitical but want to be political leaders at all fronts at the same time, sorry no offense. That includes me as well. But sometimes, it is good to do something rather than nothing.

PXA: The day Battas unite...no force can stop us from going back to Kashmir...The only humble request is please get your kids the State Subject Certificate, irrespective of whether they want to go...it keeps our doors open for next generation.

BXR: I have already done it before I left for NZ. I was surprised to know even my mother did not have one, so I got hers done as well. My State Subject is from Jammu but my grandfather had got our address as …. I will show you when we meet next.

ZXA: I have State Subject Certificate as well. However, I am not sure how does it get affected when you are not an Indian citizen.

PXA: You are an OCI holder and can still buy property in India.

KYB: … that makes you eligible to ask for Batta land in Australia.

BXR: That is where Article 370 comes to the rescue of Battas. No Indian law directly affects us. On the other note, all the agricultural land once belonged to Battas. Sheikh Abdullah took it from KPs under the Indian act of 'Land to the Tiller', that is how Muslim tillers became overnight owners of the

Pandit agricultural land. So Muslims used the Indian act to their advantage and say no to scraping Article 370.

PXA: We had around 22 kanals of land and after the act was implemented we only got Rupees 40,000.

ZXA: ...we should ask for Batta Land in Australia. The only issue is they might give us desert in Alice Springs.

BXR: That is what was given to Jews in Israel but Jews made Israel out of desert and rocky land. One of my cousin's son who went to Russia to study medicine married a Russian Jew and lives in Israel now.

PXA: *Chalo* (let us go to) Israel.

ZXA: Ironically KP story is not very different from the Jewish story of struggle. However, they finally managed to get some homeland and we still struggle.

BXR: KPs are also trying in their own way and our concern in this direction is a little step towards that realisation.

TZR: Just in case some of you forgot the history. We were called *Dal-e-Gadva* and generally shoved off. Nothing has changed. We remain wedded to *kalum* (pen), we know very little of anything else. Rights are not given on a platter.

KZR: Kashmiri Pandit's biggest tragedy is the numbers. In order for us to claim, fight or do anything substantial, we fail in numerals. That is our biggest setback. Jews were killed in the millions but many millions survived, so their case is a bit different. First, we should start reproducing. Reproducing in dozens and after three decades we will be few millions.

ZXA: Nice one KZRji. So basically *Kamasutra* is our route to homeland. Well, at least we will enjoy the journey.

KZR: *Hum do hamaare 12* (we two and our twelve children).

ZXA: Actually if you do maths, your idea is good. Within three decades, we will be about 10 million.

PXA: Is it necessary to have legal 12? Can't we sow the seeds somewhere else?

TZR: No, do you mean 10 million *Dal-e-Gadva* on this planet?

KYB: ... idea *mein hai dum*; *Aaloo khao kum* (the idea is solid; so eat less potatoes).

ZXA: *Dal Tabur* (a pot of dal).

KZR: Pray to *Shiva Lingam*.

BXR: What will be the KP country called after so many *Dal-e-Gadvas*?

KZR: The KP country should be called United States of *Haakh & Damallu*.

## References

Wakhlu S (2011), *Kashmiri Pandits–Cultural & Historical Introduction*, Gulshan Books, Srinagar, Kashmir, India.

Hassnain F (2002), *Jesus in the East*, Dastgir Publications Trust, Srinagar, Kashmir.